T0299299

Green Manufacturing for Industry 4.0

With the introduction of Industry 4.0 in manufacturing industries, the paradigm shift from conventional to green manufacturing is quite evident. Manufacturing industries achieving sustainability objectives is now the prime concern. This paradigm creates more efficient products using green processes and practices (i.e., those that produce minimal environment hazardous waste). This book provides an overview of the broad field of research on green manufacturing with a focus on the Fourth Industrial Revolution to encourage interest in the topic. It includes the dissemination of original findings on Industry 4.0 pathways and practices applied to green manufacturing development, as well as the contribution of new perspectives and roadmaps to those eager to realize the benefits of Industry 4.0 to transform the manufacturing sector into a more environment-friendly state.

This book shows how the innovations of Industry 4.0 work together to improve society, save lives, create efficiencies, and ultimately achieve the objectives of sustainability. To develop a smart green manufacturing technology, it is important to understand the prerequisites, technological developments, and technological aspects that conceptually describe this transformation. This understanding should also include practices, models, and real-world experiences. At the same time, the goal is to comprehend how Industry 4.0 technologies and smart products could result in environmental, economic, and social benefits. Essentially, the goal of this book is to provide the fundamentals of the cutting-edge smart technology-driven production maneuver known as Industry 4.0, primarily to determine and validate its potential as a practice that promotes green manufacturing to ultimately revolutionize the competitiveness of businesses and regions.

First published 2024
by Routledge
605 Third Avenue, New York, NY 10158

and by Routledge
4 Park Square, Milton Park, Abingdon, Oxon, OX14 4RN

Routledge is an imprint of the Taylor & Francis Group, an informa business

ISBN: 978-1-032-57502-5 (hbk)
ISBN: 978-1-032-57501-8 (pbk)
ISBN: 978-1-003-43968-4 (ebk)

DOI: 10.4324/9781003439684

Typeset in Garamond
by MPS Limited, Dehradun

Green Manufacturing for Industry 4.0

Building a Sustainable Future with Smart Technology

Edited by
Rityuj Singh Parihar
Naveen Jain

A PRODUCTIVITY PRESS BOOK

Contents

Preface

Humanity is at a turning point in its industrial path in the very beginning of the modern era. The convergence of technological innovation and ecological awareness has been given the name Industry 4.0, a revolutionary framework that assures not merely unusual attainment of efficiency and productivity but also an extensive revamping of manufacturing environmental sustainability.

The subject matter of this book attests to the importance and sense of urgency of such a juncture. Since the dangers of environmental degradation and exhaustion of resources have become more pressing, the need to adopt environmentally friendly manufacturing techniques is now even more severe. In these circumstances, the convergence of Industry 4.0 innovations and green manufacturing principles symbolizes an icon of optimism to a world looking for a balance between growth and conservation. It will be going via the pages which adhere to investigate the complicated interaction within the emergence of the Fourth Industrial Revolution along with the growing demand for environmentally friendly production. This collection aims to untangle the intricacies, encounter the ambiguities, and commemorate the opportunities that exist at the crossroads of each of these dominant forces.

The subject matter of this work is intended to explain the cutting-edge innovations that strengthen Industry 4.0 and illuminate their potential to transform the sustainable development of manufacturing by relying on the insights of a team of specialists, scientists, and professionals from a variety of disciplines. We explore the latest technological advances that are transforming the industry's future, from self-driving technology along with artificial intelligence, to Internet of Things and blockchain. However, our investigation expands outside the realm of philosophy. It also encompasses the real-world realm wherein these cutting-edge innovations are currently being implemented and optimized. We include standard operating procedures and real-life examples that illustrate the way Industry 4.0 has the potential to improve profitability while minimizing the adverse effects on the environment.

This work is an impassioned plea for action rather than simply a compilation of concepts. This is a call to the performers, intellectuals, and pioneers to step up and join forces in an attempt to reshape the next generation of the manufacturing process. It encourages us to dream of a future within which business flourishes not at the cost of the environment but in peaceful cooperation. We must explore the changing landscape of Industry 4.0 together with green manufacturing, using a strong sense of moral obligation and intent. Decisions that we choose now are likely to have an influence on future generations and define the lasting effects we leave behind. Let us begin this revolutionary path to an ecologically friendly and profitable future.

Dr. Rityuj Singh Parihar, Dr. Naveen Jain
Shri Shankaracharya Institute of Professional
Management and Technology, Raipur,
Chhattisgarh (INDIA) Top of Form

About the Editors

Dr. Rityuj Singh Parihar is working as an assistant professor in Mechanical Engineering Department of Shari Shankaracharya Institute of Technology Raipur, Chhattisgarh. He has completed his Ph.D. from the Department of Mechanical Engineering at National Institute of Technology Raipur in 2019. He completed his M.Tech from the Indian Institute of Technology Banaras Hindu University in 2013. His areas of research are surface engineering, finite element modeling and simulation, composites, functionally graded materials, self-lubricating material, product design and development, and Industry 4.0. He has published around 14 research articles in reputed international journals (SCI and SCOPUS) and conference proceedings. He has also published 6 book chapters and is a life member in the Institution of Mechanical Engineers.

Dr. Naveen Jain is a professor in the Mechanical Engineering Department at Shri Shankaracharya Institute of Professional Management and Technology (SSIPMT), Raipur. He holds a B.E. (Mech. Eng.) from BU; Bhopal, India, a master's degree in Production Eng. (Hons.), along with an MBA in marketing and was awarded a Ph.D. in industrial engineering from the National Institute of Technology Raipur. His research areas are sustainability, fuzzy inference systems, sustainability, SCM, MCDM, and decision modeling. He has published numerous papers in high-impact SCI/SCOPUS journals, conference proceedings, and book chapters.

Contributors

Haidar Abbas
University of Technology and
    Applied Sciences – Salalah
Salalah, Dhofar, Oman

Hafiz Wasim Akram
Dhofar University
Salalah, Oman

Fathy Yassin Alkhatib
Department of Management Science
    and Engineering, Khalifa University
Abu Dhabi, United Arab Emirates

Juman Khaldoon Alsadi
Department of Management Science
    and Engineering, Khalifa University
Abu Dhabi, United Arab Emirates

Somnath Bhattacharya
Department of Mechanical
    Engineering, National Institute of
    Technology Raipur
Raipur, Chhattisgarh, India

Ishwar Bhiradi
Department of Mechatronics,
    Manipal Institute of Technology,
    Manipal Academy of Higher
    Education
Manipal, Karnataka, India

Pardeep Bishnoi
Senior IP Analyst, Clarivate Analytics
Noida, Uttar Pradesh, India

S. Jeeva Chithambaram
Department of Civil Engineering,
    Sarala Birla University
Ranchi, Jharkhand, India

Md. Daoud Ciddikie
Sharda University
Greater Noida, Uttar Pradesh, India

Chandra Prakash Dewangan
Department of Mechanical
    Engineering, Government
    Engineering College Raipur
Raipur, Chhattisgarh, India

Pranav Gupte
Department of Industrial and
    Production Engineering, School of
    Studies of Engineering &
    Technology, Guru Ghasidas
    Central University
Bilaspur, Chhattisgarh, India

Naveen Jain
Shri Shankaracharya Institute of
  Professional Management and
  Technology
Raipur, India

Antony Jiju
Department of Management Science
  and Engineering, Khalifa
  University
Abu Dhabi, United Arab Emirates

Mohit Lal
Department of Industrial Design,
  National Institute of Technology
  Rourkela
Rourkela, Orissa, India

Harendra Kumar Narang
Department of Mechanical
  Engineering, National Institute of
  Technology Raipur
Raipur, Chhattisgarh, India

Gulab Pamnani
Department of Mechanical
  Engineering, Malaviya National
  Institute of Technology Jaipur
Jaipur, Rajasthan, India

Rityuj Singh Parihar
Department of Mechanical
  Engineering, Shri Shankaracharya
  Institute of Professional
  Management and Technology
Raipur, Chhattisgarh, India

Mariam Ali Ramadan
Department of Management Science
  and Engineering, Khalifa
  University
Abu Dhabi, United Arab Emirates

Ram Krishna Rathore
Mechanical Engineering Department,
  Rungta College of Engineering and
  Technology
Bhilai, Chhattisgarh, India

Govind Sahu
Department of Mechanical
  Engineering, Government
  Engineering College
Raipur, Chhattisgarh, India

Manish RK Sahu
Shri Shankaracharya Institute of
  Professional Management and
  Technology
Raipur, Chhattisgarh, India

Mithilesh Kumar Sahu
Department of Mechanical, OP Jindal
  University
Raigarh, Chhattisgarh, India

Vinay Sharma
Department of Production
  Engineering, Birla Institute of
  Technology
Mesra, Ranchi, Jharkhand, India

Ganesh Prasad Shukla
Department of Industrial and
 Production Engineering, School of
 Studies of Engineering &
 Technology, Guru Ghasidas
 Central University
Bilaspur, Chhattisgarh, India

Abhijeet Singh
Senior IP Analyst, Clarivate Analytics
Noida, Uttar Pradesh, India

Agnivesh Kumar Sinha
Mechanical Engineering Department,
 Rungta College of Engineering and
 Technology
Bhilai, Chhattisgarh, India

Vikas Swarnakar
Management Science and
 Engineering, Khalifa University
Abu Dhabi, United Arab Emirates

Ajay Tripathi
New Government Engineering
 College
Raipur, Chhattisgarh, India

Pratibha Sukla Tripathi
Department of Electrical and
 Electronics Engineering,
 Government Engineering College
Raipur, Chhattisgarh, India

Nitin Upadhyay
Department of Mechanical
 Engineering, Madhav Institute of
 Technology & Science
Gwalior, Madhya Pradesh, India

Neha Verma
Department of Mechanical
 Engineering, Shri Shankaracharya
 Institute of Professional
 Management and Technology
Raipur, Chhattisgarh, India

Shashikant Verma
Department of Mechanical
 Engineering, National Institute of
 Technology
Durgapur, West Bengal, India

Chapter 1

Technology-Driven Sustainability: Exploring the Synergy Between Industry 4.0 and Green Manufacturing

Pranav Gupte[1], Ganesh Prasad Shukla[1], and Vikas Swarnakar[2]

[1]Department of Industrial and Production Engineering, School of Studies of Engineering & Technology, Guru Ghasidas Central University, Bilaspur, Chhattisgarh
[2]Management Science and Engineering, Khalifa University, Abu Dhabi, United Arab Emirates

1.1 Introduction

Since the beginning of industrialization, manufacturing has been crucial in growing national economies and generating jobs [1]. The rising demand for commodities from a global population that is expanding at an increasing rate is expected to keep this trend going. However, improvements in the manufacturing industry had a negative impact on the environment, leading to disasters like global warming, the depletion of resources, inadequate handling of waste, and others. The United Nations' Agenda for 2030 enlists 17 goals for sustainable development (SDGs), three of which focus on reducing the severity of issues brought on by manufacturing processes. To achieve these goals and address environmental concerns, businesses must embrace green manufacturing (GM) methods. It addresses every stage of a product's life span, from conception to disposal, and works so in a way that is advantageous and safe, harming the environment neither significantly nor at all by maximizing resource efficiency and reducing emissions and waste [2]. Research on GM from the standpoint of operational technologies covers topics like minimizing or eliminating the use of hazardous substances, undesirable by-products, non-value-added operations, etc.

Globalization, broad customization, and a competitive business environment are forcing "traditional" enterprises to adopt novel business models and progress in the direction of the Fourth Industrial Revolution [3,4]. Manufacturing will undergo a radical change as a result of Industry 4.0 innovations, which maximize productivity and efficiency while requiring the least amount of resources [5]. Innovations in Industry 4.0 have ushered in a trend toward innovative manufacturing in industries that aimed to maximize output through effective resource utilization. Industry 4.0's "smart production" or "digital production", at its core, enables businesses for carrying out flexible manufacturing processes with high levels of modifications [6]. As per Zhong et al. [7], Industry 4.0 is a German idea that intends to build smart factories using manufacturing technologies that are changed and updated by cyber-physical systems (CPS) and the Internet of Things (IoT). Industry 4.0 production systems have the capacity to monitor industrial physical procedures and create a "digital twin" of real-world goods [8]. As a result, manufacturing organizations are encouraged to connect with machines, communicate in real time, and make wise decisions. Industry 4.0 technologies combined with smart manufacturing and embedded production systems to transform traditional organizational business models, manufacturing value chains, and industry supply chains [9]. Several key enabling technologies, such as CPS, IoT, blockchain computing, augmented and virtual reality (AR), machine learning (ML), artificial intelligence (AI), big data analytics, and digital twins can enable Industry 4.0 practices [10]. Industry 4.0 technologies are expected to promote organizational sustainability in terms of both economic performance and environmental responsibility [5]. Industry 4.0 technologies present a significant opportunity to generate sustainable value across the economic and ecological facets of sustainability by improving resource efficiency [11].

Few academics have looked at the technologies from a variety of sustainability angles, despite the likelihood that Industry 4.0 would increase manufacturing sustainability [6,10–12]. Stock and Seliger [5] emphasized GM's potential in Industry 4.0. The framework for Industry 4.0 sustainability was developed by Kamble et al. [12]. De Sousa Jabbour et al. [11] emphasized a crucial set of success traits for GM in the Industry 4.0 age. Machado et al. [6]

highlighted new research trends and prospects for GM in Industry 4.0. Sharma et al. [10] offered a bibliometric-based review to highlight the research possibilities for GM in Industry 4.0. As per Bag and Pretorius [13], there is a relationship between GM, Industry 4.0, and the circular economics. This shows that GM and Industry 4.0 are becoming more and more popular. This chapter analyzes the manufacturing research patterns across several Industry 4.0 technologies and provides the manufacturing sustainability challenges in order to better understand the prospects and research trends for sustainable production in Industry 4.0.

1.1.1 Green Manufacturing

There are numerous meanings of GM provided in the work of various researchers. The term "GM" refers to controlling the flow of environmental garbage in an effort to reduce its negative effects on the environment while simultaneously maximizing resource efficiency [14]. GM satisfies the needs of the present generation without jeopardizing the potential of future generations to satisfy their own requirements [15]. GM employs efficient production methods such source diminution, recycling, and environmentally friendly designs [16]. By implementing GM practices and design ideas, manufacturing businesses will be able to turn waste into a profitable product [17]. In addition to adopting cutting-edge practices, tools, and technology, GM lays a particular emphasis on the usage of renewable raw materials and energy. GM may have a variety of meanings for many individuals depending on their discipline and extent of training [18]. As a result, it can be said that GM is a method that reduces the environmental effect of production by reducing waste, pollution, and toxics, while also increasing productivity and profit.

With the ability to address the majority of the challenges the world faces today, green manufacturing is quickly becoming the sustainable industrial answer. The environmental characteristics of a product are mostly fixed once it enters the production line from the design stage [19]. Consequently, in order to assist the design function, tools and processes that permit an evaluation of the environmental consequences throughout each phase are needed. Understanding how business initiatives, such as green initiatives, relate to GM's environmental performance is essential. Increased industrial activity is the root cause of the global problem of adverse environmental effects. GM is presently being pursued in an effort to eliminate it entirely. Businesses have been forced to improve their environmental performance as a result of globalization's effort to make things better for the environment than ever before [20]. Consequently, the only clear choice for the current production environment is GM. The use of GM, its handling in a green manner, and recovery of resources are currently issues of the utmost concern for governments and business around the world. An organization's performance can be improved both environmentally and economically by reducing waste and emissions at the source. Thus, it is clear from the explanation earlier that GM is a significant topic that requires in-depth investigation.

1.1.2 Industry 4.0

At the 2011 Hanover show in Germany, the phrases "Industry 4.0" and "Fourth Industrial Revolution" were first used [8,21]. Industry 4.0 was formally unveiled by the German government in 2014 as the high-tech plan for German industry [6]. The term "Industry 4.0" refers to the current developments in data exchange and automation across manufacturing technologies or activities. The goal of Industry 4.0 is to build "smart" factories that can adapt to changing business models, management goals, and manufacturing conditions [4]. CPS, cloud computing, blockchain technology, AR, flexible manufacturing systems, additive manufacturing, IoT, reconfigurability, AI, cloud computing, ML, and big data analytics are some of the key enabling technologies of Industry 4.0 [22,23]. The past three generations of industrialization (Industry 1.0, Industry 2.0, and Industry 3.0), which increased resource utilization and productivity, were propelled by mechanization, electrification, and information technology in manufacturing. Industry 4.0's core technology is the CPS, which enables mass customization because to its modular structure and flexibility in production systems [12]. According to Kumar et al. [24], CPS could link physical objects, allow man-machine collaboration, facilities, processes, and other system operations when coupled to the IoT. The interaction of IoT with CPS enables communication between the physical and virtual worlds by sharing data created by industrial processes and sensor data [25]. Meanwhile, other Industry 4.0 innovations assist the commercial activities made possible by Industry 4.0.

1.1.3 Major Advantages of Industry 4.0

Manufacturers have gained an advantage over competitors by putting their strategies for Industry 4.0 innovations into action. They can embrace the forthcoming manufacturing and distribution era with modular, effective automation boosted by data-driven input, giving them full control on supply and flow of materials. Industry 4.0 has several advantages, including enhanced performance and competitiveness, increased adaptation and resilience, and increased profitability. Industry 4.0 would also enhance customer service. The advantages of Industry 4.0 ought to continue to be the main topic of every debate, despite how fascinating and invigorating Smart Factory technology is. Automation, interactions between machines, retail production, and decision-making advancements are included in this. Industry 4.0 innovations assist producers in producing better, more efficient goods. In other words, this can increase output while lowering capital costs and increasing capital reliability [26,27].

These developments allow for the democratization of data, the provision of larger perspectives, and the incorporation of Industry 4.0 and associated software. The devices will be connected as part of the "Industry 4.0" idea, establishing a connection outside the confines of the industrial facility. For many firms, data has evolved into a valuable asset. Massive amounts of well-organized data collected by sensors and other devices are very important. There is currently a goal to enhance creativity rather than replace it in the factories. The most important course of action is to invest in capacity development and culture change. The workforce could be prepared for an evolving world and made ready for additional training while remaining relevant by up skilling in analytics and novel technologies [28,29].

Utilizing these technologies across the whole value chain and expanding into external supply chain networks between organizations are also essential. It would make effective use of ML and AI from real-time information gathered throughout the supply chain while providing insightful knowledge to better judgments. Without a robust network of collaborators, such as entrepreneurs and tech businesses, who would develop readily available and affordable technologies to enable this revolution, none of this would be practical [30]. Additionally, research and development will be done in academia to advance technology. Manufacturing that is supported by Industry 4.0 may monitor, track, and track input materials and output labor via multiple production steps to efficient and precise outbound shipment. Manufacturers will have total control over the information flow and content of their plants thanks to a combination of robotics and sensors. Because customer expectations and the workplace environment are continually changing in the age of digitization, this level of control is essential for stability and efficiency [31,32].

1.2 Needs of Industry 4.0 for Nurturing Environment Sustainability

It is necessary to create a policy that enables businesses to adopt Industry 4.0 effectively. Because of the rapid development of technology and automation, it is essential to continually retrain and upgrade personnel as well as generate new jobs. Industry 4.0 is capable of performing differently in various markets and geographical areas [33]. They would consequently require a "transformative" policy on industrialization to link them to cutting-edge digital technology. It would need for an entirely new set of abilities focused on improved adaptability, the use of real-time data, and process visibility. It could be necessary to alter the line settings depending on the operator, the product, and the execution [34]. Depending on the daily requirements, repairs, or modifications needed, this may need to move aside to replenish the queue and get educated on a different procedure. Industry 4.0 is expanding, and industries across the continents are undergoing change. Emerging technological opportunities and data resources serve as the foundation for reconsidering nearly every aspect of conventional industry, including production lines, factory floors, and supply networks [35,36].

Every Industry 4.0 program requires the IoT, as does industrial IoT technology. Data collecting from a variety of devices and sensors is a component of the overall Industry 4.0 ideology, including robots in manufacturing factories, sensor dispensers in greenhouses, and systems in hospitals [37]. IoT seeks to gather data. These AI/ML applications require a huge number of enterprises to operate. Physical systems react, analyze actions using software, and monitor results. Using feedback loops, computers and networks keep track of and coordinate physical processes. The idea is to integrate devices with software where computing is used as an operation and machine learning loop rather than as the primary function [38]. Industry 4.0 is significant because its associated applications support practically all production organizations, from tiny to medium-sized businesses to huge corporations, regardless of corporate motto or language. Businesses who adopted Industry 4.0 and integrated its components into their operations have flourished [39].

1.2.1 Industry 4.0 for Green Manufacturing

The last 20 years have seen incredible advancements in a hot topic of green manufacturing. The goal of green manufacturing is to incorporate the core principles of environmental sustainability into the industrial sector. It helps to improve both economic and environmental efficiency. Industry 4.0 is an eco-technology concept that interacts with organizational and technological problems by integrating technological advancements, CPS, big data, AR, and cloud computing [40]. Green manufacturing has a lot of potential for Industry 4.0 to increase production by streamlining processes, cutting lead times, and boosting organizational effectiveness. Numerous challenges and dangers continue to face the production sector [41–43]. The majority of the technology we use on a daily basis has undergone considerable changes, and deep learning, analysis, and big data appear to be anonymous. In order to interface with machines and knowledge, some of these advances have been made more frequently and effectively. In the last 20 years, all significant businesses have embraced technology more and more, and the energy sector is no different. The only focus of technological growth is no longer the replacement of paper documents with digital electronic gadgets. The next step is to re-imagine how companies run, interact with, and work with their customers [44,45].

The concept of "Industry 4.0" is well known and blends environmentally friendly automated processes and information with a smart manufacturing environment to maximize demand, increase flexibility, and enhance performance. These developments in distributed output, green energy management, and smart grid development are all a component of the green digital transition [5]. Hardware manufacturers and software development companies have developed their skills in designing and implementing corporate applications for large-scale company processes at around the same time, emphasizing internal dependability and environmental soundness preservation. Digitization offers businesses the chance to create cutting-edge models for enterprises, renewable energy generation, and energy supply plans as prices drop and technology advances substantially [46,47].

1.2.2 Aspects of Industry 4.0 Supporting Green Manufacturing

A number of crucial components that make up the Industry 4.0 framework for fostering green manufacturing are shown in Figure 1.1. Some of the important Industry 4.0 sustainability traits are energy, materials, natural resources, waste, and emissions [48]. Under the heading of resources, the utility of water, land, and recyclability are subcategories; under the heading of energy, loss rate and utilization are subcategories; under the heading of materials, scrap rate, method used, and smart processes; and under the heading of waste and

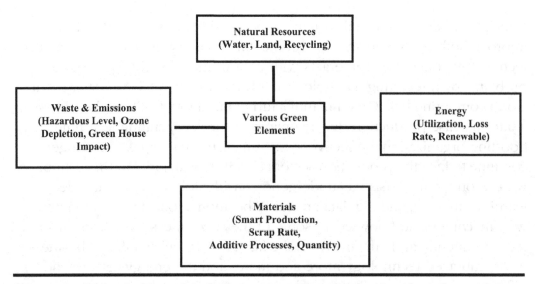

Figure 1.1 Using Industry 4.0 elements to promote Green Manufacturing.
Source: Courtesy of Javaid et al. (2022) [see 55].

emissions, detrimental level, depletion of the ozone layer, and greenhouse gas consequences are subcategories. The establishment of a sustainable ecosystem is further aided by the right continuance of these traits [49,50]. A healthy society makes use of its financial, human, and environmental resources to meet current needs and guarantee adequate resources for future generations. With the advent of Industry 4.0, work is done mostly in technologically advanced machinery and equipment in factories and other production facilities [51]. This situation makes us reflect on the value and place of individuals in the workplace. For many years, additive manufacturing has contributed significantly to advancement. Innovations have been around for a while, yet implementations were frequently restricted to prototype [52]. Small- and medium-sized manufacturing has recently experienced an upsurge of innovation and application that extends beyond engineering and design. Manufacturers have made it clear that they anticipate many ideas and solutions to be open source as the Industrial IoT continues to spread throughout the global manufacturing industry [53,54]. Waste, time, and energy are reduced with the effective application of Industry 4.0 technology, which also contributes to the development of a smart production system.

It is also vital to keep in mind that some industries, like the pharmaceutical and medical industries, require plastic packaging. Automation and modular electronics, two examples of Industry 4.0 technology, have helped to develop plastic production methods that minimize water consumption and rapid wastewater cleansing, considerably lowering the effects of plastics on water systems [56]. The use of computer-simulated realities can improve industrial manufacturing procedures. With multiple immersive innovations, it becomes simpler to manage resources, especially tools and tasks. Increased realism facilitates accurate inventory management. An employee will utilize a smartphone to identify a needed component at a sizable warehouse. AI will also use navigation to find the quickest route to move a component to another area of the industry. Additionally, it would improve worker productivity and encourage adherence to intricate processes. Many different individual interests are taken into account in a sustainable society and efficiently serviced. Every industry has a decision-making table there, giving it a safe haven for different cultures and points of view [57–59].

1.3 Industry 4.0 Components and Tools for Advancing Green Manufacturing

The key Industry 4.0 instruments for environmental sustainability domains are the Internet of Things, cloud computing, numerous Industry 4.0 principles, aspects of associated products and processes, etc. [11]. Figure 1.2 highlights the various Industry 4.0 paradigm tools for encouraging green production. Under the correct conditions, Industry 4.0 tooling and strategy can enable sustainable environment development [60]. Additional specifics on these particular components include compatibility, real-time networks, big data and immediate information, life cycle assessment, smart production, the use of sensors, digitization, etc. [61–63].

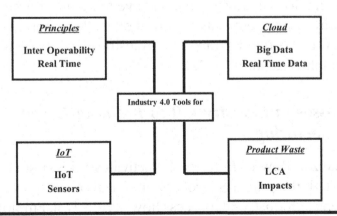

Figure 1.2   Tools specific to Industry 4.0 for embracing Green Manufacturing.
Source: Courtesy of Javaid et al. (2022) [see 55].

With new technical developments like IoT, artificial intelligence, big data, etc., the current business will alter. Artificial intelligence (AI) is one of the fundamental components of Industry 4.0 that enables robots to think, learn, and make decisions. Since the beginning of time, people have sought to increase their power and ability. These tools offer dependable technology for cutting-edge research [64,65]. The IoT is another development in technology that enables computer-human interaction. With IoT, manufacturing can be relocated to intelligent villages, towns, and cities, as well as to intelligent homes and cars. Extensive data analysis is a key component of Industry 4.0. Its major purpose is to gather feedback and information from clients so that businesses may provide them with goods and services. Resources and time are saved since it offers acceptable on-time services [66,67].

The global economy is being significantly impacted by Industry 4.0, which is also altering the economy's fundamentals. Engineers use the system's big data analytics findings to make judgments. This information prioritizes changes and actions to be performed to stop unscheduled machine downtime [68]. Big data analysis enables predictive maintenance, which drastically reduces reaction time. Another way that businesses employ big data analysis is through the automated process of supply chain management. This implies a decrease in the amount of human input and activity needed in the production process [69]. Physical modifications to equipment are automated using actuators and sophisticated robotics linked with control tools, while historical records of a manufacturing chain are reviewed and connected to current performance information. Without requiring human input, the control program uses big data analytics to give these robotics and actuators exact commands that change the actual configuration of machinery and equipment. In actuality, technological advancements have tended to be progressive, and historical upheavals have typically occurred over a long period of time. Or, to put it another way, it's the first time that industries have been integrated with modern cyber infrastructure [70–72].

1.3.1 Processes in Industry 4.0 to Promote Green Manufacturing

The conceptualized flow of Industry 4.0 activities achieving green manufacturing is depicted in Figure 1.3. Process optimization and sustainable results are the key steps in Industry 4.0 process flow sectors [73]. Employing digitized

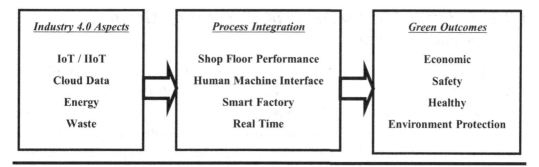

Figure 1.3   The flow of process for green manufacturing in Industry 4.0.

Source: Courtesy of Javaid et al. (2022) [see 55].

and smart dimensions is the first step, which also makes efficient and environmentally friendly culture possible everywhere. The key components for the manufacturing of environmentally friendly products are clever innovations in methods and processes. Integration is concerned with the interaction between humans and machines and how it relates to virtualization and real-time management in smart factories [6,74,75]. The economic, safety, operator health, and environmental protection aspects of sustainability all improved in various ways.

Even in highly advanced manufacturing, production can be improved and anchored by intelligent means. The so-called manufacturers' revolution has seen a number of practical innovators capitalize on the propensity to link innovation with manufacturing. It promises a more efficient form of production that frequently involves environmentally friendly procedures, remanufactured equipment, recycled products, and organic inputs [76]. By using alternative energy sources and energy-efficient lighting, machinery, and equipment, harmful emissions are decreased in sustainable production. Many consumers' shopping experiences are frequently improved as a result [77,78]. Even more ways that Industry 4.0 improves consumer services and daily life include the deployment of sophisticated robotics to boost industrial productivity and give end customers better devices. Additive manufacturing enables easy material customization to create novel structures and forms with less materials and waste [79]. The Industry 4.0 philosophy includes reduced resource use, a zero-waste effort in an era of digital circular marketplace, and a completely different approach to product creation and supply networks. Moisture, temperature, and various other relevant factors are now detected by sensors in spray rooms; as a result, whenever a change happens in how a machine operates, the accompanying environmental parameters likewise depart from the ideal setting [80].

1.3.2 Industry 4.0 Developments Supporting Green Manufacturing

The Internet of Things (IoT) and the Internet of Services are two examples of cyber-physical systems that Industry 4.0 combines with the most recent developments in industrial technology. Despite the fact that computers have historically been employed in manufacturing, this transition focuses on the cognitive collaboration, decision-making processes and interconnectedness of operations without the intervention of humans [81]. Industry 4.0 seeks to transform the current service, architectural, and production processes. This has been utilized for years by operators and distributors to lower uncertainty and improve performance. Change is made possible by both green organizational ideals and a green workforce. Utilizing Industry 4.0 technologies, green logistics systems and networks are created. Digitalization of the machinery results in technological advancements and a modernization of the environment. Successive organizational excellence can only be attained in this manner [82]. Overall effectiveness and production maintenance are achieved via Industry 4.0. Adaptive engineering, autonomous robotics, more accurate data, big data analysis, cloud computing, cybersecurity, and the convergence of horizontal and vertical device types are some examples of digital changes. Green technology and Industry 4.0 can be combined to provide information sharing and communication amongst efficient maintenance systems [83]. Specialists can make decisions in today's market-critical situations with the use of experience and research. The machine may be programmed to predict problems, reorganize itself, and adjust to change with the right study. Prediction management would entail tracking large data continuously in real-time and issuing notifications based on prediction methods like regression analysis [84,85].

Digital solutions are crucial for efficient factory setup because they allow for the combination of the benefits of a classic continuous production approach with the consistency of a flexible assembly. We can respond to customer needs considerably more quickly because to our enhanced versatility [86]. Compared to the standard conveyor system, it also requires less investment. Lack of basic supplies, environmental damage, and climate change pose ongoing threats to industries that depend on natural resources for production. As stated by Goswami and Daultani [87] in their report, their long-term goal is to find sustainable solutions that promote economic growth without further environmental degradation. Industry 4.0 has a positive effect through generating sustainable value through organized methodologies, including sustainable production strategies at the systems, process, and product levels. This necessitates for nearly a continuous circulation of close-loop materials throughout the manufacturing process via effective management of waste, standard practices for green manufacturing, and advancements made for sustainable industrial activities [88,89]. Technology in production makes it ethically and environmentally sound. Industrialization has addressed the stigma linked with the ecological balance of our various environments.

1.4 Functions of Industry 4.0 for Green Manufacturing

Industry 4.0 combines digital technologies with established operating and production procedures. Businesses may utilize instantaneous processing of data and ML to boost efficiency, improve workflows, and encourage innovation [90]. The era of sustainable production will eventually arrive with the help of Industry 4.0 technologies. Digital manufacturing increases efficiency, effectiveness, adaptability, and dependability, resulting in more successful and long-lasting organizations. Manufacturers are driven to make investments in smart manufacturing by potential increases in production volumes and efficiency as well as decreased overhead, functional, and capital costs [91]. Additionally, there are benefits of sustainability for both employees and the environment, including better quality of life, enhanced productivity of resources and energy, the use of sustainable infrastructure, and worker health and safety. The important ways that Industry 4.0 is being used to promote environmental sustainability are covered in Table 1.1.

The advantages of smart production, both qualitatively and quantitatively, can therefore be better understood using Industry 4.0. Component packing and product shipping are supported by these, which lowers delivery times and costs while also speeding up delivery. To address the majority of problems and add value to plant operations, the network working basis must be as robust, safe, and future-proof as feasible [152]. As a single infrastructure able to support extensive, delicate, and industrial automation applications, 5G technologies have a lot of potential. The Fourth Industrial era is being set in motion by advanced cellular IoT and cyber-physical networks enabled by 5G [153,154]. The IoT can increase industrial production and help us comprehend the effects of climate change. The advent of Industry 4.0 coincides with the decade that will be the most important for addressing climate change [155]. IoT deployment would become much more superficial with improved 5G networking. One innovative technological concept we are putting into practice on the plant floor is the employment of remote experts [156,157]. Virtual reality can be used to interact with and troubleshoot an on-site professional.

Table 1.1 Industry 4.0 Applications for Embracing Green Manufacturing

S.No	Applications	Overview	References
1.	Green automated facilities	As more companies reconfigure their production processes to be more eco-friendly and sustainable, Industry 4.0 is becoming increasingly common in the automated factories of the future. The cornerstone of the world economy is the manufacturing sector in a number of ways. A commercial organization might search deeper for AI-enabled energy systems, industrial IoT devices, and connected factory equipment. Industry 4.0 technologies make it possible to develop and consume responsibly with the intention of doing more. Through the circular economy and climate awareness, we, as a worldwide organization, supervise the efficient use of ecological assets and natural resources.	[78,92–94]
2.	Lower carbon footprint and lessening of pollution	The manufacturers in adjacent industries have improved in terms of reducing plastic, carbon footprint, and water pollution. It depends on Industry 4.0 technologies including digitalization, robots, renewable energy, data collecting and forecasting, IoT, and data analytics. It is not essential to use conventional fossil fuels, energy, or garbage in order to produce goods. Institutes for research and development use applications of these technologies. The ensuing research and development focuses on lightweight materials, energy safety, and solar energy use.	[4,95,96]
3.	Using digital information to improve the environment	This includes the products and services provided by the corporation in addition to the use of digital technology for communication and information to reduce the negative ecological impact of other economic sectors. Instances of related manufacturing processes have been discovered, investigated, and used in a number of industries to illustrate and quantify the advantages of smart manufacturing. It has begun an ambitious technological transformation initiative to boost operational productivity, employee safety and health, and collaboration with the product design unit to ensure design coherence with the production process.	[97–100]

4.	Increased sustainability benefits	These innovations create a comprehensive strategy for handling the intricacy of technological advances, production, and sustainability impact assessment in order to maximize the sustainability benefits of smart manufacturing. Manufacturing processes were examined and categorized based on enabling technologies and characteristics such as 5G wireless connectivity, the IoT, AI, and AR. The transformation of new concepts into practical use cases enhanced commerce, sustainability, and interoperability among manufacturers, suppliers, and consumers.	[101–104]
5.	Management of services	By connecting measurement devices, manufacturing businesses' entire information and automation network in energy and product management, Industry 4.0 is made possible. Expansions of the ability to collect, send, and store enormous volumes of data regarding the manufacturing processes, use, and transformation of energy sources. Specialized artificial intelligence algorithms can more readily recognize and analyze interest patterns across a variety of industries because of the rise of information and greater availability of computing power.	[105–108]
6.	Productivity growth	Increased profitability, marketability, and total investment are the main goals of Industry 4.0. The benefits are immediate and may result in a cycle of acquisition, success, and reinvestment. Increased financial performance is a result of increased competitiveness, and the additional funds on hand can increase capacity and productivity. One of the fundamental tenets of Industry 4.0 is the control of energy. This is utilized by proactive organizations to utilize resources and services well. Furthermore, a more demanding and fragmented market would necessitate integrating multiple power generation sources.	[109–112]
7.	Improvement in green innovation	Utilizing Industry 4.0, the most recent automation and industrial collaboration topic covers all environmental improvements. Knowledge exchanges between humans and machines have improved automated factories' workflows, boosted productivity, and decreased waste generation. A network of wired objects, including	[113–116]

(continued)

Table 1.1 (Continued) Industry 4.0 Applications for Embracing Green Manufacturing

S.No	Applications	Overview	References
		computers, sensors, actuators, and equipment, known as the IoT collects and disseminates data. A virtual representation of real-world aspects and dynamics, such as systems, equipment, processes, and physical attributes, is known as a "digital twin." Future planning, data gathering, device surveillance, and many more services can be provided by digital twins. Cyber-physical systems are recognized to incorporate advances in computing, network, physical, and environmental processes.	
8.	Optimal output	The way the cloud computing network functions together gives the impression that it is a single entity to outsiders. This information can be utilized, among other things, to reduce downtime and optimize output. Interoperability makes it possible for knowledge to be freely and efficiently transferred to every component, actuator, sensor, machine, instrument, and users. Machines and other systems in industries are frequently run via cloud computing systems. The huge and dynamic data sets that are made available from many sources of machine learning technologies are referred to as big data and analytics. Industry 4.0 creates methods, ideas, and techniques that improve safety and productivity in several sectors of the economy. The focus is on prevention tactics that may be incorporated into programs from the start, while also updating old systems to meet modern safety standards.	[117–120]
9.	Improving automation through competence and flexibility.	Systems for training and preparation are required to aid in the development of skills necessary for accomplishment in Industry 4.0 vocations. This offers improved business solutions and guarantees the workforce required for potential jobs by including opportunities for academic and vocational training. Over the past few centuries, the business and industrial sectors have undergone numerous technological revolutions. Industry 4.0 already has a lot of technical	[121–126]

#	Name	Description	Reference
		components; thus, the revolution combines products, systems, and computers. Robots are a crucial component of flexible automation and are utilized in a wide range of industrial production applications, from plasma cutting and welding to assembling and finishing. If used effectively, robot systems can improve quality control, a safe working environment, reduce bottlenecks, boost productivity, raise worker satisfaction, and more.	
10.	Ecologically sound	Increased degrees of automation boost output while enhancing worker security. Heavy machinery may now be operated via haptic feedback and remote control over 5G. This has the power to both save lives and improve the environment. As a result, mining operations and safety have improved, and new IoT use cases have been realized, including remote control of machinery, automation of ventilation systems, and real-time crew and vehicle monitoring.	[127–129]
11.	Response to climate change	This offers useful tactics and resources for tackling climate change and other sustainability-related issues, having a positive effect on industries. The exponential road map enables collaboration between scientists, tech entrepreneurs, big business, and nonprofits. The world economy is on the verge of a turning moment. New consumer prospects and changes in company practices are being brought about by the quick development of digital technology. By offering novel business strategies and boosting safety, inclusion, cost-effectiveness, and steady development for all stakeholders, it can also have a substantial impact on the future sustainability of economies.	[130–133]
12.	Managing all industrial tasks	The importance of having access to the most recent data must be recognized by industries considering automation to assist them to manage entire industrial functions. All relevant data is accessible whenever it is required with an organization's connection to cloud storage. By combining cameras and sensors, engineers may gather more data to aid in more efficiently completing their tasks. It can give the product's complete assembly instructions so that production engineers can show the maintenance crew the problems on the shop	[134–136]

(continued)

Table 1.1 (Continued) Industry 4.0 Applications for Embracing Green Manufacturing

S.No	Applications	Overview	References
		floor in real time. The integration of 3D printing and nanotechnology into supply chains and manufacturing processes has increased production flexibility and improved energy efficiency.	
13.	Reducing the waste	The automotive sector enthusiastically embraced green practices. Producers can spend less on everything from packaging and electricity to raw materials by using green production. In addition to increasing industry growth and profitability, addressing climate change offers the possibility to promote sustainability and green development. An efficient production system appears to be created when low-cost sensors are concentrated and integrated with big data analysis. These developments give suppliers novel ideas on how to streamline their production procedures and supply networks for lower costs and better customer service. Smart production techniques reduce wastage and emissions of greenhouse gases along the route, whether on purpose or by accident.	[137–139]
14.	Rapid detection and resolution of several issues	Time to market and new product development durations have significantly improved in the majority of industries. For the business and manufacturing, it leads in significant cost reductions. This new degree of information may enable the development of new products, preventive upkeep, and the quick detection and elimination of problems. However, it is impossible for businesses to deal with any of these problems independently due to the wide range of accessible methodologies and applications and the absence of unified laws. By integrating high-quality software assets and sector-specific statistics, sustainability advisory services assist businesses of all sizes and sectors in managing their individual ecological sustainability requirements. Based on discrete manufacturing, these technologies have the potential to alter the production floor.	[140–143]

| 15. | Boost market effectiveness | The linkages and complexity of sustainable production are covered by overlapping zones, position, and categorized elements of diverse processes by methodical and economical waste management in order to increase market efficiency and modelling. Progressive firms employ renewable energy sources in the manufacturing, distributing, and supply chain operations for the power sector and new innovations. Additionally, organizations employ innovative strategies and technologies to improve energy usage, eliminate waste, and increase efficiency. | [144–147] |
| 16. | Recycles waste products | Internal waste material usage, prolonged and repetitive usage of raw materials through recycling, and interconnected markets for distinct by-products are all practices that support sustainable manufacturing methods. Efficiency has increased in many industrial settings where corporations have enhanced their ecological manufacturing strategies. Industry 4.0 refers to improvements in resource utilization in production made possible by robots using vast amounts of data. Due to the wider range of services available, this enhances working conditions and even health care. | [148–151] |

1.5 Discussions

The shift detection/projective analysis, streamlined processes, new market models, higher engineering investments, and expanded industry cooperation are all ways through which Industry 4.0 reaffirms the digital revolution. Here, data may be collected using ever-improving methods, allowing studies to be conducted by adding cutting-edge instrumentation technology and scrutinizing manufacturing procedures. In energy and utility management, advanced physical instruments can now examine physical quantities, comprehend processes, and measure factors ranging from applied control. This transformation in the production and distribution of products and amenities is being driven by advancements in data analytics and networking. The IoT, AI, AR, and other technological advancements have changed the connections between people, objects, and data. Regarding technical benefits, Industry 4.0 presents a special chance to use and integrate value into the overall business strategy. Industry 4.0 is a phenomenon that has already had a significant impact on a number of industries, ranging from manufacturing to customer service, all over the world. The opportunity to deploy Industry 4.0 has never been greater.

Digital designs can be produced utilizing Industry 4.0 technology and related software. These designs are built on personalized knowledge. It is all too easy to see the problems that could arise from errors in the production, marketing, and packing industries. It is crucial to keep an eye out and conduct exacting tests and controls appropriate for Industry 4.0 technologies. One of the main benefits of the early changes in manufacturing was the ability to produce extras of the same goods when leveraging economies of scale. The duty of this supply is crucial for mechanical makers. Industry 4.0 intends to offer the precise answers needed. Unbelievably simple and versatile design and manufacturing are made possible by intelligent plants with integrated workflows that have been digitally developed for any product. The main application techniques are involved with input, in-process components, finished goods, inventory management, measurement, and evaluation. The end consequence is that good results can be achieved by ensuring and improving the consistency of the processes and products. It is possible to achieve rapid and long-term growth by digitalizing integrated production procedures. Decentralization, interoperability, and virtualization are the finest actions that organizations can take to reduce errors and extra costs. IoT-enabled hardware and sensors transmit real-time information directly to the engineers' computers and other relevant devices. Notifications will be sent through apps when maintenance or repairs are required. Engineers may use production line data to monitor and improve procedures. IoT supports manufacturing engineers in their decision-making. Using computerized analytical tools and procedures, big data can reveal recurrent trends, commonalities, and correlations. Big data analysis is being used more by business leaders to identify systems that need to be changed. It makes improvements to help with effective production processes.

The Fourth Industrial Revolution, known as "Industry 4.0", will enable a number of production sectors to become more environmentally friendly. Since smart factories generate enormous volumes of data, a data analyst, an AI expert, and a big data professional are needed to manage the data, gain ideas from it, optimize processes and equipment, and keep the factory running. This recognizes a chance and prepares us for new duties by utilizing new technology. Data can nearly always be used to draw conclusions. Without digitization, it was previously difficult to monitor and get information on business models and manufacturing costs. A few factors that prevented the industry from operating efficiently included a lack of resources, high power needs, and a lack of energy. AI, ML, and automation have made it easier for manufacturers to learn about all of these issues and work toward creating an industrial facility that can manage power, supplies, and energy restrictions. This would help enterprises become more reliable and competitive while also sharply reducing manufacturing costs. It is now our duty to make the best possible use of this stage of industrialization in order to build a more important, goal-oriented, and environmentally sound society. With the use of Industry 4.0 technology, this system aims to provide direction and guidance for the environmental values. It concentrated on determining which sustainability issues are crucial for an organization to address.

1.6 Future Implications

The term "Industry 5.0" refers to an emerging paradigm that has improved communication and collaboration between people and machinery. Industry 4.0's summary of the evolution of cyber-physical networks has evolved into

Industry 5.0, fundamentally altering how we live, work, and connect. The laws governing our interactions with one another and with machines must be defined in the next technology revolution. As automation, AI, and even robot work records support the employees and take control over sizable areas of production, delivery, and processes, the degree of collaboration between humans and technology will change. The quick pace of change puts a strain on all employees, governments, legislators, and regulators. Industry 5.0 is credited with demonstrating the value of engaging individuals in the process. To keep up with growing demand, manufacturers will be compelled to adopt technology for services including product production, customization, and after-sale service.

Flexible production, improved efficiency, and the introduction of new business models will all be made possible by digital solutions. However, there is even greater hope for the manufacturing sector in the future, which will create new opportunities for both distinct and process sectors to cater to the particular requirements of their clients. The digital industries make it possible for businesses of all kinds to streamline and digitize their operational procedures. Digitization can begin at any point along a corporation's value chain. The digital twin is produced as a result of design of a new production facility, the development of an innovative item, and its manufacturing. Industry 4.0 technologies enable more rapid and effective innovation while using significantly fewer resources. 5G networks provide the latency that businesses need for both present and upcoming systems, in addition to flexibility. Latency is a critical component of numerous applications related to Industry 4.0 as well as any form of factory automation activity. Industry 4.0 will continue to gain popularity and importance in the manufacturing sector for a number of reasons. Industry 4.0, to put it simply, is the forthcoming era of technology development that will drive operational effectiveness. The technologies of Industry 4.0 will be progressively adopted by businesses for a number of reasons. Modern operational technology will benefit manufacturers by helping them minimize delays, enhance efficiency, and lower the overall expenses of producing components of superior quality. Preemptive repair techniques, machine surveillance software, and other functional advancements are all included in this technology.

1.7 Conclusions

Digital automation of tasks requiring green energy is one of the key areas that Industry 4.0 advancements may enhance. Industries such as mining, oil, and gas all leverage IoT solutions to achieve the functional efficiency objectives of the energy business. Data analysis and robotics are some of these solutions. Digitalization is having a positive impact on smart logistics and is advantageous to many businesses. A healthy ecosystem is made possible by the use of drones and IoT devices for the examination of production lines and facilities. Integrated grid meters can be used to access detailed statistics on gas, fuel, electricity, and water usage. Additionally, IoT systems might be able to recognize variations in moisture, temperature, and vibration, reducing system breakdowns and improving human safety. A digital twin enables a company to track crucial success metrics using information gathered via IoT technologies connected to its physical twin. The goal of data integration in ML systems is to alert operators for probable problems, anticipate costs, and provide ecologically conscious options. A theoretically limitless amount of production information can be processed in the cloud utilizing digital data for a sustainable functioning platform. Innovative technology makes it possible to convert the manual data gathering method into a digital gathering mechanism, which will then be utilized to train new employees to design sophisticated algorithms by using techniques that have already been established. The manufacturer will have to act quickly to address future difficulties like the skills gap, shifting consumer demand, and new product trends.

References

1. Shukla, G. P., & Adil, G. K. (2021). A conceptual four-stage maturity model of a firm's green manufacturing technology alternatives and performance measures. *Journal of Manufacturing Technology Management, 32*(7), 1444–1465. 10.1108/JMTM-09-2020-0368
2. Rehman, M. A., & Shrivastava, R. L. (2013). Green manufacturing (GM): Past, present and future (a state of art review). *World Review of Science, Technology and Sustainable Development, 10*(1-2-3), 17–55. 10.1504/WRSTSD.2013.050784
3. Aiello, G., Giallanza, A., Vacante, S., Fasoli, S., & Mascarella, G. (2020). Propulsion monitoring system for digitized ship management: Preliminary results from a case study. *Procedia Manufacturing, 42*, 16–23. 10.1016/j.promfg.2020.02.018
4. Oztemel, E., & Gursev, S. (2020). Literature review of Industry 4.0 and related technologies. *Journal of Intelligent Manufacturing, 31*, 127–182. 10.1007/s10845-018-1433-8
5. Stock, T., & Seliger, G. (2016). Opportunities of sustainable manufacturing in Industry 4.0. *Procedia CIRP, 40*, 536–541. 10.1016/j.procir.2016.01.129

6. Machado, C. G., Winroth, M. P., & Ribeiro da Silva, E. H. D. (2020). Sustainable manufacturing in Industry 4.0: An emerging research agenda. *International Journal of Production Research*, *58*(5), 1462–1484. 10.1080/00207543.2019.1652777

7. Zhong, R. Y., Xu, X., Klotz, E., & Newman, S. T. (2017). Intelligent manufacturing in the context of Industry 4.0: A review. *Engineering*, *3*(5), 616–630. 10.1016/J.ENG.2017.05.015

8. Kim, J. H. (2017). A review of cyber-physical system research relevant to the emerging IT trends: Industry 4.0, IoT, big data, and cloud computing. *Journal of Industrial Integration and Management*, *2*(03), 1750011. 10.1142/S2424862217500117

9. Ejsmont, K., Gladysz, B., & Kluczek, A. (2020). Impact of Industry 4.0 on sustainability—Bibliometric literature review. *Sustainability*, *12*(14), 5650. 10.3390/su12145650

10. Sharma, R., Jabbour, C. J. C., & Lopes de Sousa Jabbour, A. B. (2021). Sustainable manufacturing and Industry 4.0: What we know and what we don't. *Journal of Enterprise Information Management*, *34*(1), 230–266. 10.1108/JEIM-01-2020-0024

11. de Sousa Jabbour, A. B. L., Jabbour, C. J. C., Foropon, C., & Godinho Filho, M. (2018). When titans meet–Can Industry 4.0 revolutionise the environmentally-sustainable manufacturing wave? The role of critical success factors. *Technological Forecasting and Social Change*, *132*, 18–25. 10.1016/j.techfore.2018.01.017

12. Kamble, S. S., Gunasekaran, A., & Gawankar, S. A. (2018). Sustainable Industry 4.0 framework: A systematic literature review identifying the current trends and future perspectives. *Process Safety and Environmental Protection*, *117*, 408–425. 10.1016/j.psep.2018.05.009

13. Bag, S., & Pretorius, J. H. C. (2022). Relationships between Industry 4.0, sustainable manufacturing and circular economy: Proposal of a research framework. *International Journal of Organizational Analysis*, *30*(4), 864–898. 10.1108/IJOA-04-2020-2120

14. Devika, K., Shankar, K. M., & Gholipour, P. (2022). Paving the way for a green transition through mitigation of green manufacturing challenges: A systematic literature review. *Journal of Cleaner Production*, *368*, 132578. 10.1016/j.jclepro.2022.132578

15. Saxena, A., & Srivastava, A. (2022). Industry application of green manufacturing: A critical review. *Journal of Sustainability and Environmental Management*, *1*(1), 32–45. 10.5281/zenodo.6207141

16. Ghadimi, P., O'Neill, S., Wang, C., & Sutherland, J. W. (2021). Analysis of enablers on the successful implementation of green manufacturing for Irish SMEs. *Journal of Manufacturing Technology Management*, *32*(1), 85–109. 10.1108/JMTM-10-2019-0382

17. Hassan, A. S., & Jaaron, A. A. (2021). Total quality management for enhancing organizational performance: The mediating role of green manufacturing

practices. *Journal of Cleaner Production*, *308*, 127366. 10.1016/j.jclepro.2021. 127366

18. Naim, A., Muniasamy, A., Clementking, A., & Rajkumar, R. (2022). Relevance of green manufacturing and IoT in industrial transformation and marketing management. In *Computational Intelligence Techniques for Green Smart Cities* (pp. 395–419). Cham: Springer International Publishing. 10.1007/978-3-030-96429-0_19

19. Zhang, H. C., Kuo, T. C., Lu, H., & Huang, S. H. (1997). Environmentally conscious design and manufacturing: A state-of-the-art survey. *Journal of Manufacturing Systems*, *16*(5), 352–371. 10.1016/S0278-6125(97)88465-8

20. Zhu, Q., Sarkis, J., & Lai, K. H. (2007). Green supply chain management: pressures, practices and performance within the Chinese automobile industry. *Journal of Cleaner Production*, *15*(11-12), 1041–1052. 10.1016/j.jclepro. 2006.05.021

21. Ching, N. T., Ghobakhloo, M., Iranmanesh, M., Maroufkhani, P., & Asadi, S. (2022). Industry 4.0 applications for sustainable manufacturing: A systematic literature review and a roadmap to sustainable development. *Journal of Cleaner Production*, *334*, 130133. 10.1016/j.jclepro.2021.130133

22. Gupta, A., & Randhawa, P. (2022). Implementing Industry 4.0 and sustainable manufacturing: Leading to smart factory. In *Industry 4.0 and Advanced Manufacturing: Proceedings of I-4AM 2022* (pp. 471–482). Singapore: Springer Nature Singapore. 10.1007/978-981-19-0561-2_41

23. Gadekar, R., Sarkar, B., & Gadekar, A. (2022). Investigating the relationship among Industry 4.0 drivers, adoption, risks reduction, and sustainable organizational performance in manufacturing industries: An empirical study. *Sustainable Production and Consumption*, *31*, 670–692. 10.1016/j.spc.2022. 03.010

24. Kumar, V., Vrat, P., & Shankar, R. (2022). Factors influencing the implementation of Industry 4.0 for sustainability in manufacturing. *Global Journal of Flexible Systems Management*, *23*(4), 453–478. 10.1007/s40171-022-00312-1

25. Verma, P., Kumar, V., Daim, T., Sharma, N. K., & Mittal, A. (2022). Identifying and prioritizing impediments of Industry 4.0 to sustainable digital manufacturing: A mixed method approach. *Journal of Cleaner Production*, *356*, 131639. 10.1016/j.jclepro.2022.131639

26. Müller, J. M., Kiel, D., & Voigt, K. I. (2018). What drives the implementation of Industry 4.0? The role of opportunities and challenges in the context of sustainability. *Sustainability*, *10*(1), 247. 10.3390/su10010247

27. Jamwal, A., Agrawal, R., Sharma, M., Kumar, V., & Kumar, S. (2021). Developing A sustainability framework for Industry 4.0. *Procedia CIRP*, *98*, 430–435. 10.1016/j.procir.2021.01.129

28. Miśkiewicz, R., & Wolniak, R. (2020). Practical application of the Industry 4.0 concept in a steel company. *Sustainability*, *12*(14), 5776. 10.3390/su12145776

30. Moshood, T. D. (2020). Emerging challenges and sustainability of Industry 4.0 era in the Malaysian construction industry. *International Journal of Recent Technology and Engineering*, *4*, 1627–1634. 10.35940/ijrte.A2564.059120

29. Vrchota, J., Pech, M., Rolinek, L., & Bednář, J. (2020). Sustainability outcomes of green processes in relation to Industry 4.0 in manufacturing: Systematic review. *Sustainability*, *12*(15), 5968. 10.3390/su12155968

31. Margherita, E. G., & Braccini, A. M. (2020). Organizational impacts on sustainability of Industry 4.0: A systematic literature review from empirical case studies. In *Digital Business Transformation: Organizing, Managing and Controlling in the Information Age* (pp. 173–186). Springer International Publishing. 10.1007/978-3-030-47355-6_12

32. Moktadir, M. A., Ali, S. M., Kusi-Sarpong, S., & Shaikh, M. A. A. (2018). Assessing challenges for implementing Industry 4.0: Implications for process safety and environmental protection. *Process Safety and Environmental Protection*, *117*, 730–741. 10.1016/j.psep.2018.04.020

33. Beier, G., Ullrich, A., Niehoff, S., Reißig, M., & Habich, M. (2020). Industry 4.0: How it is defined from a sociotechnical perspective and how much sustainability it includes–A literature review. *Journal of Cleaner Production*, *259*, 120856. 10.1016/j.jclepro.2020.120856

34. Habib, M. K., & Chimsom, C. (2019, May). Industry 4.0: Sustainability and design principles. In *2019 20th International Conference on Research and Education in Mechatronics (REM)* (pp. 1–8). IEEE. 10.1109/REM.2019.8744120

35. Varela, L., Araújo, A., Ávila, P., Castro, H., & Putnik, G. (2019). Evaluation of the relation between lean manufacturing, Industry 4.0, and sustainability. *Sustainability*, *11*(5), 1439. 10.3390/su11051439

36. Ivanov, D., & Ivanov, D. (2018). New drivers for supply chain structural dynamics and resilience: Sustainability, Industry 4.0, self-adaptation. *Structural Dynamics and Resilience in Supply Chain Risk Management*, 293–313. 10.1007/978-3-319-69305-7_10

37. Ammar, M., Haleem, A., Javaid, M., Walia, R., & Bahl, S. (2021). Improving material quality management and manufacturing organizations system through Industry 4.0 technologies. *Materials Today: Proceedings*, *45*(6), 5089–5096. 10.1016/j.matpr.2021.01.585

38. Birkel, H. S., Veile, J. W., Müller, J. M., Hartmann, E., & Voigt, K. I. (2019). Development of a risk framework for Industry 4.0 in the context of sustainability for established manufacturers. *Sustainability*, *11*(2), 384. 10.3390/su11020384

39. Bhagawati, M. T., Manavalan, E., Jayakrishna, K., & Venkumar, P. (2019). Identifying key success factors of sustainability in supply chain management for Industry 4.0 using DEMATEL method. In *Proceedings of International Conference on Intelligent Manufacturing and Automation: ICIMA 2018* (pp. 583–591). Springer Singapore. 10.1007/978-981-13-2490-1_54

40. Piccarozzi, M., Aquilani, B., & Gatti, C. (2018). Industry 4.0 in management studies: A systematic literature review. *Sustainability*, *10*(10), 3821. 10.3390/su10103821

41. Saniuk, S., Grabowska, S., & Gajdzik, B. (2020). Social expectations and market changes in the context of developing the Industry 4.0 concept. *Sustainability*, *12*(4), 1362. 10.3390/su12041362

42. Martínez-Olvera, C., & Mora-Vargas, J. (2019). A comprehensive framework for the analysis of Industry 4.0 value domains. *Sustainability*, *11*(10), 2960. 10.3390/su11102960

43. Dossou, P. E. (2018). Impact of Sustainability on the supply chain 4.0 performance. *Procedia Manufacturing*, *17*, 452–459. 10.1016/j.promfg.2018. 10.069

44. Chong, S., Pan, G. T., Chin, J., Show, P. L., Yang, T. C. K., & Huang, C. M. (2018). Integration of 3D printing and Industry 4.0 into engineering teaching. *Sustainability*, *10*(11), 3960. 10.3390/su10113960

45. Dalenogare, L. S., Benitez, G. B., Ayala, N. F., & Frank, A. G. (2018). The expected contribution of Industry 4.0 technologies for industrial performance. *International Journal of Production Economics*, *204*, 383–394. 10.1016/j.ijpe. 2018.08.019

46. Junior, J. A. G., Busso, C. M., Gobbo, S. C. O., & Carreão, H. (2018). Making the links among environmental protection, process safety, and Industry 4.0. *Process Safety and Environmental Protection*, *117*, 372–382. 10.1016/j.psep. 2018.05.017

47. Mendoza-del Villar, L., Oliva-Lopez, E., Luis-Pineda, O., Benešová, A., Tupa, J., & Garza-Reyes, J. A. (2020). Fostering economic growth, social inclusion & sustainability in Industry 4.0: A systemic approach. *Procedia Manufacturing*, *51*, 1755–1762. 10.1016/j.promfg.2020.10.244

48. Sajid, S., Haleem, A., Bahl, S., Javaid, M., Goyal, T., & Mittal, M. (2021). Data science applications for predictive maintenance and materials science in context to Industry 4.0. *Materials Today: Proceedings*, *45*(6), 4898–4905. 10. 1016/j.matpr.2021.01.357

49. Stachová, K., Papula, J., Stacho, Z., & Kohnová, L. (2019). External partnerships in employee education and development as the key to facing Industry 4.0 challenges. *Sustainability*, *11*(2), 345. 10.3390/su11020345

50. Abbasi, A., & Kamal, M. M. (2020). Adopting Industry 4.0 technologies in citizens' electronic-engagement considering sustainability development. In *Information Systems: 16th European, Mediterranean, and Middle Eastern Conference, EMCIS 2019, Dubai, United Arab Emirates, December 9–10, 2019, Proceedings 16* (pp. 304–313). Springer International Publishing. 10.1007/978-3-030-44322-1_23

51. Prause, M. (2019). Challenges of Industry 4.0 technology adoption for SMEs: The case of Japan. *Sustainability*, *11*(20), 5807. 10.3390/su11205807

52. Lin, K. C., Shyu, J. Z., & Ding, K. (2017). A cross-strait comparison of innovation policy under Industry 4.0 and sustainability development transition. *Sustainability*, *9*(5), 786. 10.3390/su9050786

53. Manavalan, E., & Jayakrishna, K. (2019). A review of Internet of Things (IoT) embedded sustainable supply chain for Industry 4.0 requirements. *Computers & Industrial Engineering*, *127*, 925–953. 10.1016/j.cie.2018.11.030

54. Garcia-Muiña, F. E., González-Sánchez, R., Ferrari, A. M., & Settembre-Blundo, D. (2018). The paradigms of Industry 4.0 and circular economy as enabling drivers for the competitiveness of businesses and territories:

The case of an Italian ceramic tiles manufacturing company. *Social Sciences,* *7*(12), 255. 10.3390/socsci7120255

55. Javaid, M., Haleem, A., Singh, R. P., Suman, R., & Gonzalez, E. S. (2022). Understanding the adoption of Industry 4.0 technologies in improving environmental sustainability. *Sustainable Operations and Computers, 3,* 203–217. 10.1016/j.susoc.2022.01.008

56. Müller, J. M., & Voigt, K. I. (2018). Sustainable industrial value creation in SMEs: A comparison between Industry 4.0 and made in China 2025. *International Journal of Precision Engineering and Manufacturing-Green Technology, 5,* 659–670. 10.1007/s40684-018-0056-z

57. Morrar, R., Arman, H., & Mousa, S. (2017). The fourth industrial revolution (Industry 4.0): A social innovation perspective. *Technology Innovation Management Review, 7*(11), 12–20.

58. Ashima, R., Haleem, A., Bahl, S., Javaid, M., Mahla, S. K., & Singh, S. (2021). Automation and manufacturing of smart materials in additive manufacturing technologies using Internet of Things toward the adoption of Industry 4.0. *Materials Today: Proceedings, 45*(6), 5081–5088. 10.1016/j.matpr.2021.01.583

59. Stock, T., Obenaus, M., Kunz, S., & Kohl, H. (2018). Industry 4.0 as enabler for a sustainable development: A qualitative assessment of its ecological and social potential. *Process Safety and Environmental Protection, 118,* 254–267. 10.1016/j.procir.2016.01.129

60. Ahmad, S., Miskon, S., Alabdan, R., & Tlili, I. (2020). toward sustainable textile and apparel industry: Exploring the role of business intelligence systems in the era of Industry 4.0. *Sustainability, 12*(7), 2632. 10.3390/su12072632

61. Haleem, A., Vaishya, R., Javaid, M., & Khan, I. H. (2020). Artificial Intelligence (AI) applications in orthopaedics: An innovative technology to embrace. *Journal of Clinical Orthopaedics and Trauma, 11*(Suppl 1), S80. 10.1016%2Fj. jcot.2019.06.012

62. Khanzode, A. G., Sarma, P. R. S., Mangla, S. K., & Yuan, H. (2021). Modeling the Industry 4.0 adoption for sustainable production in micro, small & medium enterprises. *Journal of Cleaner Production, 279,* 123489. 10.1016/ j.jclepro.2020.123489

63. Yadav, G., Luthra, S., Jakhar, S. K., Mangla, S. K., & Rai, D. P. (2020). A framework to overcome sustainable supply chain challenges through solution measures of Industry 4.0 and circular economy: An automotive case. *Journal of Cleaner Production, 254,* 120112. 10.1016/j.jclepro.2020.120112

64. Pham, T. T., Kuo, T. C., Tseng, M. L., Tan, R. R., Tan, K., Ika, D. S., & Lin, C. J. (2019). Industry 4.0 to accelerate the circular economy: A case study of electric scooter sharing. *Sustainability, 11*(23), 6661. 10.3390/su11236661

65. Paravizo, E., Chaim, O. C., Braatz, D., Muschard, B., & Rozenfeld, H. (2018). Exploring gamification to support manufacturing education on Industry 4.0 as an enabler for innovation and sustainability. *Procedia Manufacturing, 21,* 438–445. 10.1016/j.promfg.2018.02.142

66. Tseng, M. L., Tan, R. R., Chiu, A. S., Chien, C. F., & Kuo, T. C. (2018). Circular economy meets Industry 4.0: Can big data drive industrial symbiosis?. *Resources, Conservation and Recycling, 131*, 146–147. 10.1016/j.resconrec.2017.12.028

67. Tirabeni, L., De Bernardi, P., Forliano, C., & Franco, M. (2019). How can organisations and business models lead to a more sustainable society? A framework from a systematic review of the Industry 4.0. *Sustainability, 11*(22), 6363. 10.3390/su11226363

68. Haleem, A., Javaid, M., & Khan, I. H. (2019). Current status and applications of artificial intelligence (AI) in medical field: An overview. *Current Medicine Research and Practice, 9*(6), 231–237. 10.1016/j.cmrp.2019.11.005

69. Scavarda, A., Daú, G., Scavarda, L. F., & Goyannes Gusmão Caiado, R. (2019). An analysis of the corporate social responsibility and the Industry 4.0 with focus on the youth generation: A sustainable human resource management framework. *Sustainability, 11*(18), 5130. 10.3390/su11185130

70. Fritzsche, K., Niehoff, S., & Beier, G. (2018). Industry 4.0 and climate change—Exploring the science-policy gap. *Sustainability, 10*(12), 4511. 10.3390/su10124511

71. Xu, L. D., Xu, E. L., & Li, L. (2018). Industry 4.0: State of the art and future trends. *International Journal of Production Research, 56*(8), 2941–2962. 10.1080/00207543.2018.1444806

72. Tsai, W. H., & Lu, Y. H. (2018). A framework of production planning and control with carbon tax under Industry 4.0. *Sustainability, 10*(9), 3221. 10.3390/su10093221

73. Kagermann, H. (2014). Change through digitization—Value creation in the age of Industry 4.0. In *Management of Permanent Change* (pp. 23–45). Wiesbaden: Springer Fachmedien Wiesbaden. 10.1007/978-3-658-05014-6_2

74. Ingaldi, M., & Ulewicz, R. (2019). Problems with the implementation of Industry 4.0 in enterprises from the SME sector. *Sustainability, 12*(1), 217. 10.3390/su12010217

75. Büchi, G., Cugno, M., & Castagnoli, R. (2020). Smart factory performance and Industry 4.0. *Technological Forecasting and Social Change, 150*, 119790. 10.1016/j.techfore.2019.119790

76. Godina, R., Ribeiro, I., Matos, F., T. Ferreira, B., Carvalho, H., & Peças, P. (2020). Impact assessment of additive manufacturing on sustainable business models in Industry 4.0 context. *Sustainability, 12*(17), 7066. 10.3390/su12177066

77. Prause, G., & Atari, S. (2017). On sustainable production networks for Industry 4.0. *Entrepreneurship and Sustainability Issues, 4*(4), 421–431. 10.9770/jesi.2017.4.4(2)

78. Javaid, M., & Haleem, A. (2020). Critical components of Industry 5.0 toward a successful adoption in the field of manufacturing. *Journal of Industrial Integration and Management, 5*(03), 327–348. 10.1142/S2424862220500141

79. Yin, Y., Stecke, K. E., & Li, D. (2018). The evolution of production systems from Industry 2.0 through Industry 4.0. *International Journal of Production Research, 56*(1-2), 848–861. 10.1080/00207543.2017.1403664

80. Belaud, J. P., Prioux, N., Vialle, C., & Sablayrolles, C. (2019). Big data for agri-food 4.0: Application to sustainability management for by-products supply chain. *Computers in Industry*, *111*, 41–50. 10.1016/j.compind.2019.06.006

81. Patidar, A., Sharma, M., Agrawal, R., & Sangwan, K. S. (2022). Supply chain resilience and its key performance indicators: An evaluation under Industry 4.0 and sustainability perspective. *Management of Environmental Quality: An International Journal*, *34*(4), 962–980. 10.1108/MEQ-03-2022-0091

82. Pandey, V., Sircar, A., Bist, N., Solanki, K., & Yadav, K. (2023). Accelerating the renewable energy sector through Industry 4.0: Optimization opportunities in the digital revolution. *International Journal of Innovation Studies*, *7*(2), 171–188. 10.1016/j.ijis.2023.03.003

83. Hung, H. C., & Chen, Y. W. (2023). Striving to achieve United Nations sustainable development goals of Taiwanese SMEs by adopting Industry 4.0. *Sustainability*, *15*(3), 2111. 10.3390/su15032111

84. Maculotti, G., Genta, G., & Galetto, M. (2023). Optimisation of laser welding of deep drawing steel for automotive applications by machine learning: A comparison of different techniques. *Quality and Reliability Engineering International*. 10.1002/qre.3377

85. Attri, R., & Vikas. (2023). Prioritisation of key readiness factors to adopt Industry 4.0 in manufacturing organisations using select MCDM approaches. *International Journal of Process Management and Benchmarking*, *13*(3), 303–334. 10.1504/IJPMB.2023.129610

86. Riso, T., & Morrone, C. (2023). To align technological advancement and ethical conduct: An analysis of the relationship between digital technologies and sustainable decision-making processes. *Sustainability*, *15*(3), 1911. 10. 3390/su15031911

87. Goswami, M., & Daultani, Y. (2022). Make-in-India and Industry 4.0: Technology readiness of select firms, barriers and socio-technical implications. *The TQM Journal*, *34*(6), 1485–1505. 10.1108/TQM-06-2021-0179

88. Sahoo, P., Saraf, P. K., & Uchil, R. (2022). Identification of critical success factors for leveraging Industry 4.0 technology and research agenda: A systematic literature review using PRISMA protocol. *Asia-Pacific Journal of Business Administration*, (ahead-of-print). 10.1108/APJBA-03-2022-0105

89. Labucay, I. (2022). Is there a smart sustainability transition in manufacturing? Tracking externalities in machine tools over three decades. *Sustainability*, *14*(2), 838. 10.3390/su14020838

90. Sony, M. (2018). Industry 4.0 and lean management: A proposed integration model and research propositions. *Production & Manufacturing Research*, *6*(1), 416–432. 10.1080/21693277.2018.1540949

91. Tortorella, G., Miorando, R., Caiado, R., Nascimento, D., & Portioli Staudacher, A. (2021). The mediating effect of employees' involvement on the relationship between Industry 4.0 and operational performance improvement. *Total Quality Management & Business Excellence*, *32*(1-2), 119–133. 10.1080/14783363.2018.1532789

92. M. Mabkhot, M., Ferreira, P., Maffei, A., Podržaj, P., Mądziel, M., Antonelli, D., … & Lohse, N. (2021). Mapping Industry 4.0 enabling technologies into United Nations sustainability development goals. *Sustainability, 13*(5), 2560. 10.3390/su13052560

93. Tsai, W. H., & Lai, S. Y. (2018). Green production planning and control model with ABC under Industry 4.0 for the paper industry. *Sustainability, 10*(8), 2932. 10.3390/su10082932

94. Erboz, G. (2017). How to define Industry 4.0: Main pillars of Industry 4.0. *Managerial Trends in the Development of Enterprises in Globalization Era, 761*, 761–767.

95. do Rosário Cabrita, M., & Duarte, S. (2021). Addressing sustainability and Industry 4.0 to the business model. In *Research Anthology on Cross-Industry Challenges of Industry 4.0* (pp. 818–838). IGI Global. 10.4018/978-1-7998-854 8-1.ch041

96. Samaranayake, P., Ramanathan, K., & Laosirihongthong, T. (2017, December). Implementing Industry 4.0—A technological readiness perspective. In *2017 IEEE International Conference on Industrial Engineering and Engineering Management (IEEM)* (pp. 529–533). IEEE. 10.1109/IEEM.2017.8289947

97. Santos, K., Loures, E., Piechnicki, F., & Canciglieri, O. (2017). Opportunities assessment of product development process in Industry 4.0. *Procedia Manufacturing, 11*, 1358–1365. 10.1016/j.promfg.2017.07.265

98. Branger, J., & Pang, Z. (2015). From automated home to sustainable, healthy and manufacturing home: A new story enabled by the Internet-of-Things and Industry 4.0. *Journal of Management Analytics, 2*(4), 314–332. 10.1080/232 70012.2015.1115379

99. Chalmeta, R., & Santos-deLeon, N. J. (2020). Sustainable supply chain in the era of Industry 4.0 and big data: A systematic analysis of literature and research. *Sustainability, 12*(10), 4108. 10.3390/su12104108

100. Sarkis, J., & Zhu, Q. (2018). Environmental sustainability and production: Taking the road less travelled. *International Journal of Production Research, 56*(1-2), 743–759. 10.1080/00207543.2017.1365182

101. Gerlitz, L. (2016). Design management as a domain of smart and sustainable enterprise: Business modelling for innovation and smart growth in Industry 4.0. *Entrepreneurship and Sustainability Issues, 3*(3), 244. http://dx.doi.org/ 10.9770/jesi.2016.3.3(3)

102. Takhar, S. S., & Liyanage, K. (2020). The impact of Industry 4.0 on sustainability and the circular economy reporting requirements. *International Journal of Integrated Supply Management, 13*(2-3), 107–139. 10.1504/IJISM. 2020.107845

103. Javaid, M., Haleem, A., Singh, R. P., & Suman, R. (2021). Significant applications of big data in Industry 4.0. *Journal of Industrial Integration and Management, 6*(04), 429–447. 10.1142/S2424862221500135

104. Javaid, M., & Haleem, A. (2020). Impact of Industry 4.0 to create advancements in orthopaedics. *Journal of Clinical Orthopaedics and Trauma, 11*, S491–S499. 10.1016/j.jcot.2020.03.006

105. Nahavandi, S. (2019). Industry 5.0—A human-centric solution. *Sustainability, 11*(16), 4371. 10.3390/su11164371

106. Fonseca, L., Amaral, A., & Oliveira, J. (2021). Quality 4.0: The EFQM 2020 model and Industry 4.0 relationships and implications. *Sustainability, 13*(6), 3107. 10.3390/su13063107

107. Dassisti, M., Semeraro, C., & Chimenti, M. (2019). Hybrid exergetic analysis—LCA approach and the Industry 4.0 paradigm: Assessing manufacturing sustainability in an Italian SME. *Procedia Manufacturing, 33*, 655–662. 10.1016/j.promfg.2019.04.082

108. Salimova, T., Vukovic, N., & Guskova, N. (2020). Toward sustainability through Industry 4.0 and Society 5.0. *International Review,* (3-4), 48–54.

109. Hofmann, E., & Rüsch, M. (2017). Industry 4.0 and the current status as well as future prospects on logistics. *Computers in Industry, 89*, 23–34. 10.1016/j.compind.2017.04.002

110. Tsai, W. H., Chu, P. Y., & Lee, H. L. (2019). Green activity-based costing production planning and scenario analysis for the aluminum-alloy wheel industry under Industry 4.0. *Sustainability, 11*(3), 756. 10.3390/su11030756

111. Müller, J. M., Buliga, O., & Voigt, K. I. (2018). Fortune favors the prepared: How SMEs approach business model innovations in Industry 4.0. *Technological Forecasting and Social Change, 132*, 2–17. 10.1016/j.techfore.2017.12.019

112. Wang, X. V., & Wang, L. (2019). Digital twin-based WEEE recycling, recovery and remanufacturing in the background of Industry 4.0. *International Journal of Production Research, 57*(12), 3892–3902. 10.1080/00207543.2018.1497819

113. Facchini, F., Oleśków-Szłapka, J., Ranieri, L., & Urbinati, A. (2019). A maturity model for logistics 4.0: An empirical analysis and a roadmap for future research. *Sustainability, 12*(1), 86. 10.3390/su12010086

114. Sołtysik-Piorunkiewicz, A., & Zdonek, I. (2021). How Society 5.0 and Industry 4.0 ideas shape the open data performance expectancy. *Sustainability, 13*(2), 917. 10.3390/su13020917

115. Barreto, L., Amaral, A., & Pereira, T. (2017). Industry 4.0 implications in logistics: An overview. *Procedia Manufacturing, 13*, 1245–1252. 10.1016/j.promfg.2017.09.045

116. Trappey, A. J., Trappey, C. V., Fan, C. Y., Hsu, A. P., Li, X. K., & Lee, I. J. (2017). IoT patent roadmap for smart logistic service provision in the context of Industry 4.0. *Journal of the Chinese Institute of Engineers, 40*(7), 593–602. 10.1080/02533839.2017.1362325

117. Gregori, F., Papetti, A., Pandolfi, M., Peruzzini, M., & Germani, M. (2017). Digital manufacturing systems: A framework to improve social sustainability of a production site. *Procedia CIRP, 63*, 436–442. 10.1016/j.procir.2017.03.113

118. Dallasega, P., Rauch, E., & Linder, C. (2018). Industry 4.0 as an enabler of proximity for construction supply chains: A systematic literature review. *Computers in Industry*, *99*, 205–225. 10.1016/j.compind.2018.03.039

119. Waibel, M. W., Steenkamp, L. P., Moloko, N., & Oosthuizen, G. A. (2017). Investigating the effects of smart production systems on sustainability elements. *Procedia Manufacturing*, *8*, 731–737. 10.1016/j.promfg.201 7.02.094

120. Adamik, A., & Nowicki, M. (2019). Pathologies and paradoxes of co-creation: A contribution to the discussion about corporate social responsibility in building a competitive advantage in the age of Industry 4.0. *Sustainability*, *11*(18), 4954. 10.3390/su11184954

121. Ibarra, D., Ganzarain, J., & Igartua, J. I. (2018). Business model innovation through Industry 4.0: A review. *Procedia Manufacturing*, *22*, 4–10. 10.1016/ j.promfg.2018.03.002

122. Ghafoorpoor Yazdi, P., Azizi, A., & Hashemipour, M. (2019). A hybrid methodology for validation of optimization solutions effects on manufacturing sustainability with time study and simulation approach for SMEs. *Sustainability*, *11*(5), 1454. 10.3390/su11051454

123. Mittal, S., Khan, M. A., Romero, D., & Wuest, T. (2018). A critical review of smart manufacturing & Industry 4.0 maturity models: Implications for small and medium-sized enterprises (SMEs). *Journal of Manufacturing Systems*, *49*, 194–214. 10.1016/j.jmsy.2018.10.005

124. Cotet, C. E., Deac, G. C., Deac, C. N., & Popa, C. L. (2020). An innovative Industry 4.0 cloud data transfer method for an automated waste collection system. *Sustainability*, *12*(5), 1839. 10.3390/su12051839

125. Schallock, B., Rybski, C., Jochem, R., & Kohl, H. (2018). Learning Factory for Industry 4.0 to provide future skills beyond technical training. *Procedia Manufacturing*, *23*, 27–32. 10.1016/j.promfg.2018.03.156

126. Haseeb, M., Hussain, H. I., Ślusarczyk, B., & Jermsittiparsert, K. (2019). Industry 4.0: A solution toward technology challenges of sustainable business performance. *Social Sciences*, *8*(5), 154. 10.3390/socsci8050154

127. Verma, P., Kumar, V., Bhatt, P. C., Kumar Drave, V. A., Hsu, S. C., Lai, K. K., & Pal, V. (2020). Industry 4.0 in emerging economies: Technological and societal challenges for sustainability. In *Applications and Challenges of Maintenance and Safety Engineering in Industry 4.0* (pp. 31–48). IGI Global. 10.4018/978-1-7998-3904-0.ch002

128. Salkin, C., Oner, M., Ustundag, A., & Cevikcan, E. (2018). A conceptual framework for Industry 4.0. *Industry 4.0: Managing the Digital Transformation*, 3–23. 10.1007/978-3-319-57870-5

129. Szalavetz, A. (2019). Industry 4.0 and capability development in manufacturing subsidiaries. *Technological Forecasting and Social Change*, *145*, 384–395. 10.1016/j.techfore.2018.06.027

130. Mohelska, H., & Sokolova, M. (2018). Management approaches for Industry 4.0—The organizational culture perspective. *Technological and Economic Development of Economy*, *24*(6), 2225–2240. 10.3846/tede.2018.6397

131. Oluyisola, O. E., Sgarbossa, F., & Strandhagen, J. O. (2020). Smart production planning and control: Concept, use-cases and sustainability implications. *Sustainability*, *12*(9), 3791. 10.3390/su12093791

132. Munsamy, M., & Telukdarie, A. (2018, December). Application of Industry 4.0 toward achieving business sustainability. In *2018 IEEE International Conference on Industrial Engineering and Engineering Management (IEEM)* (pp. 844–848). IEEE. 10.1109/IEEM.2018.8607566

133. Felsberger, A., & Reiner, G. (2020). Sustainable Industry 4.0 in production and operations management: A systematic literature review. *Sustainability*, *12*(19), 7982. 10.3390/su12197982

134. Müller, J. M. (2019). Antecedents to digital platform usage in Industry 4.0 by established manufacturers. *Sustainability*, *11*(4), 1121. 10.3390/su11041121

135. Dzwigol, H., Dzwigol-Barosz, M., Miśkiewicz, R., & Kwilinski, A. (2020). Manager competency assessment model in the conditions of Industry 4.0. *Entrepreneurship and Sustainability Issues*, *7*(4), 2630. 10.9770/jesi.2020. 7.4(5)

136. Ramadan, M., Salah, B., Othman, M., & Ayubali, A. A. (2020). Industry 4.0-based real-time scheduling and dispatching in lean manufacturing systems. *Sustainability*, *12*(6), 2272. 10.3390/su12062272

137. Theorin, A., Bengtsson, K., Provost, J., Lieder, M., Johnsson, C., Lundholm, T., & Lennartson, B. (2017). An event-driven manufacturing information system architecture for Industry 4.0. *International Journal of Production Research*, *55*(5), 1297–1311. 10.1080/00207543.2016.1201604

138. Alladi, T., Chamola, V., Parizi, R. M., & Choo, K. K. R. (2019). Blockchain applications for Industry 4.0 and industrial IoT: A review. *IEEE Access*, 7, 176935–176951. 10.1109/ACCESS.2019.2956748

139. Upadhyay, A., Mukhuty, S., Kumar, V., & Kazancoglu, Y. (2021). Blockchain technology and the circular economy: Implications for sustainability and social responsibility. *Journal of Cleaner Production*, *293*, 126130. 10.1016/ j.jclepro.2021.126130

140. Yang, S., MR, A. R., Kaminski, J., & Pepin, H. (2018). Opportunities for Industry 4.0 to support remanufacturing. *Applied Sciences*, *8*(7), 1177. 10.3390/app8071177

141. Rauch, E., Unterhofer, M., Rojas, R. A., Gualtieri, L., Woschank, M., & Matt, D. T. (2020). A maturity level-based assessment tool to enhance the implementation of Industry 4.0 in small and medium-sized enterprises. *Sustainability*, *12*(9), 3559. 10.3390/su12093559

142. Diez-Olivan, A., Del Ser, J., Galar, D., & Sierra, B. (2019). Data fusion and machine learning for industrial prognosis: Trends and perspectives toward Industry 4.0. *Information Fusion*, *50*, 92–111. 10.1016/j.inffus.2018.10.005

143. Pilloni, V. (2018). How data will transform industrial processes: Crowdsensing, crowdsourcing and big data as pillars of Industry 4.0. *Future Internet*, *10*(3), 24. 10.3390/fi10030024

144. Nelles, J., Kuz, S., Mertens, A., & Schlick, C. M. (2016, March). Human-centered design of assistance systems for production planning and control: The role of the human in Industry 4.0. In *2016 IEEE International Conference on Industrial Technology (ICIT)* (pp. 2099–2104). IEEE. 10.1109/ICIT.2016. 7475093

145. Fernández-Caramés, T. M., & Fraga-Lamas, P. (2018). A review on human-centered IoT-connected smart labels for the Industry 4.0. *IEEE Access, 6,* 25939–25957. 10.1109/ACCESS.2018.2833501

146. Zhang, J., Ding, G., Zou, Y., Qin, S., & Fu, J. (2019). Review of job shop scheduling research and its new perspectives under Industry 4.0. *Journal of Intelligent Manufacturing, 30,* 1809–1830. 10.1007/s10845-017-1350-2

147. Santos, C., Mehrsai, A., Barros, A. C., Araújo, M., & Ares, E. (2017). Toward Industry 4.0: An overview of European strategic roadmaps. *Procedia Manufacturing, 13,* 972–979. 10.1016/j.promfg.2017.09.093

148. Di Carlo, F., Mazzuto, G., Bevilacqua, M., & Ciarapica, F. E. (2021). Retrofitting a process plant in an Industry 4.0 perspective for improving safety and maintenance performance. *Sustainability, 13*(2), 646. 10.3390/su1302 0646

149. Chen, M., Sinha, A., Hu, K., & Shah, M. I. (2021). Impact of technological innovation on energy efficiency in Industry 4.0 era: Moderation of shadow economy in sustainable development. *Technological Forecasting and Social Change, 164,* 120521. 10.1016/j.techfore.2020.120521

150. Elsisi, M., Tran, M. Q., Mahmoud, K., Lehtonen, M., & Darwish, M. M. (2021). Deep learning-based Industry 4.0 and Internet of Things toward effective energy management for smart buildings. *Sensors, 21*(4), 1038. 10.3390/ s21041038

151. Batkovskiy, A. M., Leonov, A. V., Pronin, A. Y., Semenova, E. G., Fomina, A. V., & Balashov, V. M. (2019). Sustainable development of Industry 4.0: The case of high-tech products system design. *Entrepreneurship and Sustainability Issues, 6*(4), 1823. 10.9770/jesi.2019.6.4(20)

152. Marques, M., Agostinho, C., Zacharewicz, G., & Jardim-Gonçalves, R. (2017). Decentralized decision support for intelligent manufacturing in Industry 4.0. *Journal of Ambient Intelligence and Smart Environments, 9*(3), 299–313. 10.3233/AIS-170436

153. Trstenjak, M., Opetuk, T., Cajner, H., & Tosanovic, N. (2020). Process planning in Industry 4.0—Current state, potential and management of transformation. *Sustainability, 12*(15), 5878. 10.3390/su12155878

154. Çınar, Z. M., Abdussalam Nuhu, A., Zeeshan, Q., Korhan, O., Asmael, M., & Safaei, B. (2020). Machine learning in predictive maintenance toward sustainable smart manufacturing in Industry 4.0. *Sustainability, 12*(19), 8211. 10.3390/su12198211

155. Narula, S., Puppala, H., Kumar, A., Frederico, G. F., Dwivedy, M., Prakash, S., & Talwar, V. (2021). Applicability of Industry 4.0 technologies in the adoption

of global reporting initiative standards for achieving sustainability. *Journal of Cleaner Production, 305*, 127141. 10.1016/j.jclepro.2021.127141

156. Lim, C. H., Lim, S., How, B. S., Ng, W. P. Q., Ngan, S. L., Leong, W. D., & Lam, H. L. (2021). A review of Industry 4.0 revolution potential in a sustainable and renewable palm oil industry: HAZOP approach. *Renewable and Sustainable Energy Reviews, 135*, 110223. 10.1016/j.rser.2020.110223

157. Enyoghasi, C., & Badurdeen, F. (2021). Industry 4.0 for sustainable manufacturing: Opportunities at the product, process, and system levels. *Resources, Conservation and Recycling, 166*, 105362. 10.1016/j.resconrec. 2020.105362

Chapter 2

State of Art Technologies in Industry 4.0 for Green Manufacturing

Rityuj Singh Parihar[1], Neha Verma[1], Vinay Sharma[2], and Mohit Lal[3]

[1]*Department of Mechanical Engineering, Shri Shankaracharya Institute of Professional Management and Technology, Raipur, Chhattisgarh, India*
[2]*Department of Production Engineering, Birla Institute of Technology, Mesra, Ranchi, Jharkhand, India*
[3]*Department of Industrial Design, National Institute of Technology Rourkela, Rourkela, Orissa, India*

2.1 Introduction

In the last 20 years, people all over humanity have become fascinated by Industry 4.0. However, current globalization faces numerous challenges in meeting the world's ever-increasing demand for consumer and capital goods and simultaneously preserving social and economic sustainability. Now, progress toward the fourth phase of the Industrial Revolution, known as Industry 4.0, is primarily shaping the creation of industrial value in developed countries. As a result, Industry 4.0 it is not solely concerning production but about the way many different products, operations, projects, communities, and enterprises operating as a result of the collaboration of software, hardware, machine learning (ML), artificial intelligence (AI), and humans. Industry 4.0 offers freedom for the implementation and acceptance of

DOI: 10.4324/9781003439684-2

sustainable production. In the twenty-first-century Fourth Industrial Revolution known as Industry 4.0, autonomous systems bring together the Internet of Things (IOT) and manufacturing practices to steer smart processes. Also, modern innovations like additive, AI, and robotics assist these practices to reach their maximum effectiveness through enabling self-customization and self-optimization [1].

Without impacting significantly the planet's present state and boosting the principle of livelihood and functioning, then fostering the evolution of a community, results in sustainable development. In short, it's growth that caters to the needs of today's generation without affecting the needs of upcoming generations to ensure they are able to utilize the resources that we're blessed with now. The real purpose of sustainable development is going to be accomplished only by creating an appropriate balance among planet (nature or resources), people, world organization, and organizational regulations. The ultimate objective of sustainable development cannot be achieved if any of the three elements is missing [2].

Humanity faces many challenges in ensuring that all people have equal opportunities for development. Consequently, objectives of sustainable growth are to cover all dimensions of social fairness, social progress, environmental safety, natural resource protection, and stability, as well as steady economic progress. These goals will be met by reducing poverty, unemployment, and environmental pollution. Also, the harmony among destruction and the conservation of the environment is always needed, which we comprehend as a critical component to the environmental and economic growth of all countries. Though Industry 4.0 has revealed several innovations to humanity, and chances for technological advances in production as well as improvement have grown significantly, the question of environment protection still remains. How will new business models affect environment, and how will they offer to place the coming generations of the humanities under the spotlight? Thus, multiple significant technologies that contribute to the realization of Industry 4.0 are briefly discussed in what follows.

2.2 Essential Technology Innovation for Industry 4.0

The contribution of technological innovation leads to the realization of Industry 4.0. In this era of digitization, numerous important inventions are key elements in Industry 4.0. They are given in Figure 2.1 and elaborated briefly in following sections.

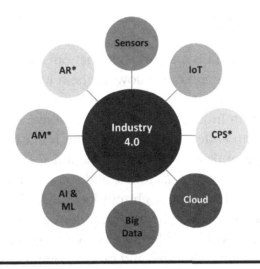

Figure 2.1 Essential elements required for the realization of Industry 4.0. (*AR: Augmented Reality; *AM: Additive Manufacturing; *CPS: Cyber Physical System.)

2.2.1 Sensors and Actuators

One of the key elements of Industry 4.0 is sensors. Sensors help mechanical devices make sense. The sensor could sense, monitor, and assess the state of a machine's operation in an effective way. Sensors detect and produce data of machine working and contextual information. Various types of sensors are adopted in the manufacturing enterprise for measurement of various physical variables. Radio-frequency identification (RFID) is a widely used sensor for object localization and identification. RFID technology enables the embedding of small quantity data in tag form. These tags are electromagnetic radio wave sensitive and can be identified by the data embedded within them. RFID tags have several advantages, such as flexibility in application, smaller size, reusable, and readable by an RFID reader in close proximity without visualization or physical contact. RFID is categorized into two kinds: long-range RFID, or RAIN RFID, and vicinity RFID.

Actuators are electromechanical or mechanical parts of a system or machine that allow the system's mechanisms to be moved and controlled. The actuator generates movement (which are small and can be rotational or linear) by converting fluidic, air, or electrical energy. Actuators are widely utilized in the manufacturing business to operate heavy machinery. It enables extremely accurate movement and control of a system or machinery [1,2].

2.2.2 *Internet of Things*

The Internet of Things (IoT) is a technology that offered connection among everyday items through the internet, allowing them to communicate with one another by exchanging data. IoT is used for connectivity among various entities or mechanical devices in Industry 4.0 to form a massive network that transfers data between devices and offers intelligent facilities for fast decision making. IoT connects a wide range of diverse cyber-physical articles or things, such as automobiles, appliances, services, factories, and so on to the internet in order to advance manufacturing ability. Through transitional gateway nodes such as routers, modems, and switches, cyber-physical devices can transfer and share data using standard protocols in different environments. Incorporation of humans, intelligent machines, sensors, and production processes makes a system which is networked intelligent, as well as agile, and it is called the Internet of Everything or Internet of Service or Internet of Manufacturing Services.

Three major elements of the IoT system are embedded systems, i.e., collection of diverse sensors that provide info about a physical article. Another element is middleware, which is in charge of acquisition control, network connectivity, and data aggregation. One more element is cloud services. The IoT can integrate numerous devices proficient in communication, networking, sensing, and actuation, and in that way develop new opportunities for manufacturing business [3,4].

Additionally, the Industrial IoT (IIoT) introduces a plethora of computing, sensing, networking, and storing capabilities, all of them critical components of Industry 4.0. Well-organized AI technology and microprocessors empower smart machinery and products having control, computing, and communication abilities, and autonomy through sociality. Within IIoT, ML is integrated through grids, clouds, and clusters for large data storage, process, and analyses. Furthermore devices in IIoT constantly generating and transmitting data streams, resulting in increased data traffic in the network between device-cloud communication. Big data analytics is becoming a significant contributor to improving intelligence across the IIoT. The main elements of the IIoT are sensing systems, outer gateway processors, inner gateway processors, outer central processors, and inner central processors.

2.2.3 *Cyber-Physical System*

Cyber-physical system (CPS) is a method of interacting, connecting, and managing different devices and computer application linked to the internet and users. Software and physical components in CPS function at diverse temporal, spatial, and behavioral scales and interact with one another in a variety of situations. As computing technology advances, mechanical systems (devices) evolve and become more automatic. A computer and a computer-based algorithm are used to control, coordinate, and monitor mechanical systems (machines) in CPS. Both systems are inextricably linked via the internet and users. Computer instructs the mechanical systems to complete the task, followed by feedback processing to computer for assessment. To achieve maximum job efficiency, computers calibrate the algorithm based on feedback. CPS increases the efficiency of job processing and adds an intellect of automation. CPS is a concept that extends the embedded system concept, wherein computation is performed through separate devices. CPS is intended to be a network of cooperating computational and physical devices. Mechatronics' data and information processing power is gradually trans-forming the outdated shop floor into an environment for elastic, reconfigur-able, scalable, network-enabled collaboration between allotted embedded equipment and business processes. 5G architecture, a five-level CPS structure, was proposed as a CPS construction standard. These five levels are smart connection level, data-to-information conversion level, cyber level, cognition level, and configuration [5].

2.2.4 *Cloud Computing*

IoT, AI, big data, and cloud computing are empowering features of Industry 4.0, with a prime focus on industry computerization. Cloud computing has significantly advanced information technology (IT) in the last 20 years, with required self-service, universal network admittance, quick elasticity, and resource pooling. Clouds having infrastructure super-vision capabilities are a collection of easily functioning and accessible virtual reserves such as various development platforms, services, hardware, and applications that can be reconstituted to permit self-service and best reserve consumption. Cloud computing is computing services on the internet at a requirement. It includes servers, networking storage, software, databases, intelligence, analytics, and so on. It is infrastructure backing for facilities (hardware, software, and platform), offering internet use by private or public organizations. Productivity, performance, cost, speed, and scal-ability are beneficial for the production of industry in meeting up with varying computation needs [6,7].

2.2.5 Edge/Fog Computing

Manufacturing enterprise necessitates on-time computation and cannot rely on a cloud-based computation. The fog computing model divests most computation necessity from cloud and fetches it nearer to IoT devices to reduce latency. Fog computing supports the usage of devices such as switches, routers, set-top boxes, base stations, Wi-Fi access points, and so on in adjacent proximity to sensors. Fog computing enables improved data processing along with better output. The "smart factory" concept is empowered via operational technology and enables software and hardware to observe or make variation in events and processes by direct detection and/or control by integrated IT with IIoT. Devices connected by these means can observe, record, analyze, and transfer data that can be utilized to control and examine manufacturing conditions. Further data collected using these devices is applied for smart decision taking, knowledge mining, and estimation to achieve accurate, efficient, and economic manufacturing [8].

Cloud computing is extended to the edge computation via fog computing. Fog performs closely with IoT actuators and sensors to create and apply data. Fog computing mainly decentralizes digital resources such as applications, networking, and data edge devices from distant data centers. The cloud must be enriched by offering computing-plus-networking supplies to edge nodes to minimize service delivery delays and communication. Edge computing deals alongside separated edge nodes, while fog computing relies on node-linking abilities. Edge computing is driven by a handful of top-down sections that frequently share with basic protocol gateway operations, and the fog links the devices and data existent in the edge in cloud-to-sensor, function-to-function, or peer-to-peer hierarchies [9].

2.2.6 Pervasive and Ubiquitous Computing

This is a networked computing framework that allows the setting up of computation and sensing equipment in practical applications, alongside the objective of rendering every computation and non-computing machines interconnected and smart. Individuals are able to access needed data and computation wherever and whenever they might require it because of a growing number of ubiquitous devices. Data is gathered by tiny low-power systems and spread to be processed by the ubiquitous system. The ubiquitous computing detects both the user's and the surrounding's circumstances prior to carrying out the intended estimation to offer the data necessary or action.

Ubiquitous computing looks in ways that things in the real world connect to themselves along with individuals [10].

2.2.7 High-speed Wireless Networks

A wireless network links more than one device (computers) to communicate wirelessly. This type of network is extensively utilized for linking different IoT and ubiquitous equipment, permitting access to networks to be easy and affordable. Manufacturing facilities are overcrowded with machinery, making it hard to join all equipment (such as sensors and computation equipment) across a network that is wired. The issue deteriorates if the wired connection collapses or new devices have to be linked to the present system. A wireless network permits a variety of equipment to link together swiftly and effortlessly without incurring the costs of network infrastructure arrangement and repairs. Wireless networks, on the other hand, are actually less efficient compared to wired ones, and this leads to an issue with transfer of data. Wireless networks, on the other hand, are somewhat less efficient compared to wired networks, leading to an obstruction (packet drop) with transmission of data once a sensor or another ubiquitous/IoT gadget creates an excessive quantity of information at a rapid pace. A rapid connectivity wireless network would make life much easier and is a must to establish Industry 4.0 norms. Wireless technology for transmission is capable of linking robots, devices, or employees, all while enhancing adaptability through decreasing and stream-lining wiring in ready-to-use systems. The networking structures offers very low latencies, substantial stability, low energy consumption, extremely low costs for communication, as well as effective transmission of information and administration.

2.2.8 Big Data Analytics

Big data analytics is a sophisticated data collection and analysis process that uncovers significant findings or details encoded in huge amounts of data. Analytics on big data can offer beneficial commercial and informative perspectives [11].

2.2.9 AI and ML

AI and ML both gather and examine data, turning it into insights and data that can be employed to create accurate operation strategies. ML is an artificial intelligence tool that prepares devices to acquire knowledge and make smart choices. The algorithms used for machine learning allow devices to acquire knowledge and find concealed details or perspectives in sets of data.

2.2.10 Cognitive Computing

Cognitive computing is a platform for technology that employs AI to make computing more intelligent. The use of cognitive computing reproduces human thought processes in order to address complicated issues, especially those that are vague or unresolved. Cognitive computing stands out by its capacity to acquire knowledge. The computing model advances its ability to make choices by learning from previous experiences [12].

2.2.11 Augmented Reality

It is a computer-assisted interactive and virtual representation that involves actual events, surroundings, or elements wherein computers enhance or impose perceptual data over objects in the real world. Video, audio, graphics, animation, and images appear as superimposed sections of content on real-world items, and simulated contact and suggestions are employed for interactions, supplying a better user experience. As an outcome, virtual reality improves one's understanding of tangible things [13].

2.2.12 Additive Manufacturing

Another name for additive manufacturing is 3D printing. It describes the procedure of constructing elements by layering material. This transforming method of production enables the development of both lighter and stronger objects. This technology enables the creation of a broad range of intricate forms without requiring individual part assembly or welding [14].

2.2.13 Allied Technologies

As an outcome of Industry 4.0, numerous sophisticated technologies depicted in Figure 2.2 for production that have been strongly associated with universal manufacturing facilities have come to light. The following part addresses several of these innovations.

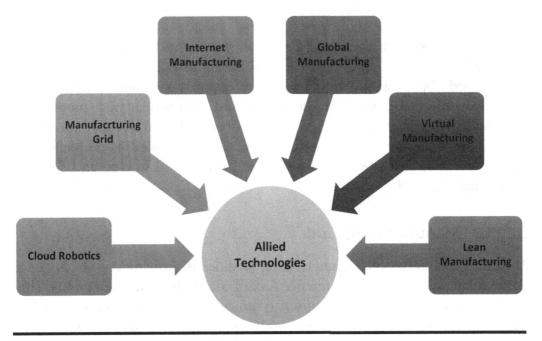

Figure 2.2   Key allied technologies for Industry 4.0.

2.2.13.1 Cloud Robotics

Robots have been used for decades to assist humans in performing several challenging tasks in an effective and accurate approach. They are mainly employed in manufacturing facilities to carry out laborious, monotonous, or hazardous duties in an accurate way. The implementation of robots offers competitive benefits by enhancing the quality of products and reducing cost per item while ensuring security for workers. The connected robot system provides a scenario wherein the robots are linked via wireless or wired networking structures and have the capability to offer a wider range of functionalities. They can share information within themselves while working in a collaborative setting to finish a task.

Cloud robotics is an emerging field in robotics which possesses the ability to advance outside networked robotics. In networked robotics, computational abilities have limitations by the individual robots, and data sharing is limited to the network. Because of innovations in cloud computing, cloud-based robotics possesses the ability to eradicate several such barriers while offering greater intelligence, effective, and economically viable solutions. In cloud-based robotics, the complex computing procedure is sent to the cloud platform via communication networks, lowering the amount of computation required for individual robots.

With the progress of Industry 4.0, the acceptance of cloud robotics across multiple with exploring unidentified circumstances and necessitates an advanced on-board computing facility. In the industrial scenario, gripping unidentified objects with extreme accuracy requires enormous information processing and computation in the foreground. In a similar way, plenty of parameters need to be considered while global and local navigation require enormous computing and storage capacity. Cloud robotics fits perfectly in such application fields because of its huge cloud-based storage and computing ability [15].

2.2.13.2 Manufacturing Grid

The complexity of goods manufacturing facilities is growing day by day as a consequence of consumer preference for affordable and excellent goods. This demand necessitates business houses to utilize their own capacities as well as supplies accessible somewhere else, using networks. Grid technology is now gaining momentum in scientific computation, management of databases, and collaborative projects. Manufacturing grid (MGrid) is an emerging idea in the realm of manufacturing. The main idea behind MGrid is to manage various kinds of resources dispersed across various geographic areas, businesses, and other organizations. MGrid is now offering users easier access to a range of manufacturing-related services like never before. By means of networking, it may assist enterprises with specialized manufacturing requirements. The consumer believes that every resource can be obtained regionally, regardless of diversity and geographic/regional allocation of resources. MGrid intends to render it simpler to businesses as well as users to access numerous manufacturing assistance over the internet.

2.2.13.3 Internet Manufacturing

Industry 4.0 refers to the evolution of an innovative digital industrial revolution supported by multiple advances in technology such as cyberse-curity, cloud computing, big data analytics, IoT, and so on. Sensors, IT systems, machines, and workpieces connect to each other in this atmosphere via the internet, which spans multiple regions. Interaction among intercon-nected devices takes place via normal internet protocols, and they have the potential of adapting to desired change, self-configuration, and failure estimation. The objective of internet manufacturing, commonly referred to as cyber manufacturing, is to improve the manufacturing of superior products at more affordable prices. Cyber manufacturing employs a methodical approach to production processes that incorporates internet technology to accomplish an enterprise's functional goal of higher efficiency and fewer interruptions. It outperforms its predecessor, e-manufacturing, in terms of scalability, learning ability, accessibility, and so on. Lack of norms, cybersecurity, and big data handling are some of the issues that must be dealt with in order to promote internet manufacturing as more common as well as acceptable in the industry.

2.2.13.4 Global Manufacturing

A global manufacturing system can be described as an entity that produces different parts, finished products, and assemblies for a different organization by using raw materials, cost, infrastructure, and an efficient supply chain network that stretches throughout the world. Manufacturing units situated in multiple regions of the globe need networking to streamline manufacturing and other associated activities. Their global reach and collaboration allow them to remain on top of their regional rivals in respect to pricing, service, and technological advances. In global manufacturing, an association of companies' groups is responsible for purchasing, production, and transportation operations instead of just one unit. The existence of omnipresent high-bandwidth connectivity to the internet opens a path for global manufacturing to develop a robust supply chain management network [16].

2.2.13.5 Virtual Manufacturing

The virtual manufacturing process is revolutionizing the manufacturing industry. It is a manufacturing process that employs a computer-aided design circumstance. It uses virtual reality to create a computer-simulated environment of the real-world manufacturing procedure. It can provide an improved comprehension of a procedure without a requirement to prototype models, save time in the process and product development cycle, and reduce wasted materials and flawed design. Furthermore, when compared to a traditional production system, the virtual manufacturing process trains an operator who is unfamiliar swiftly, reducing machine time waste. The virtual manufacturing environment is backed with many kinds of web-based technologies. Web-based virtual systems are currently accessible for use with machine tool design, tool performance evaluation, and every step of production. Web-based CAM subsystems that have the ability exhibit the ongoing manufacturing procedure that has been established to animate different stages of manufacturing [17].

2.2.13.6 Lean Manufacturing

Lean manufacturing is an organized strategy to minimize waste during manufacturing while preserving capacity and quality. It operates tirelessly to eliminate waste from the production procedure. Toyota Motor Corporation has successfully employed lean manufacturing in past years, showing a substantial rise in efficiency and a reduction in waste in the company's operation. Other manufacturing companies around the globe are now using the method of lean manufacturing in order to boost productivity through minimizing waste. The adoption of lean technology is fraught with numerous difficulties and obstacles, such as effective collaboration, surveillance, cooperation, and so on; as an outcome, some industries have accomplished only limited or insufficient success. Integration of lean manufacturing in Industry 4.0 has long been a research priority. Automation in manufacturing has served a significant role in this collaboration. The execution problems related to lean manufacturing in the industry involving customer, supplier, control, and process, and human factors have already been thoroughly solved using technologies linked to Industry 4.0 [5].

2.3 Conclusion

Manufacturing technological advances have paved the way for a new industrial revolution. Industry 4.0 refers to this new paradigm shift. Numerous governments around the world are attempting to bolster their manufacturing facilities and, as a result, increase the size of their markets. Cyber-physical systems, the Internet of Things, big data, and cloud computing are assisting industries and manufacturing units in transitioning to a new industrial paradigm. Industrial structures are being created to ensure the effective execution of the new manufacturing ecosystem. The Industrial Internet of Things is a collection of physical objects, structures, applications, and stages that use embedded development to grant and communicate information to one another, the external environment, and people. The improved availability and sensitivity of processors, sensors, and different innovations that allowed for receipt as well as access to consistent information are driving the allocation of industrial IoT. The IIoT and Industry 4.0 remain "fluffy" concepts. Because these concepts lack precise and widely accepted definitions, we presented some that logical writing deemed important. IIoT can provide critical benefits to organizations in a broad spectrum of industries. For example, rather than focusing solely on specialized difficulties, the relationships among every stakeholder, from individuals to companies to governance, should be considered. Businesses and governments have to bolster their efforts and raise their expectations in the coming years, but they must also change their approaches to training, competencies, and function.

References

1. Pramanik, P. K. D., Pal, S. and Choudhury, P. (2019). "Smartphone Crowd Computing: A Rational Solution toward Minimising the Environmental Externalities of the Growing Computing Demands," In Emerging Trends in Disruptive Technology Management, R. Das, M. Banerjee and S. De, Eds., CRC Press.
2. Pramanik, P. K. D., Mukherjee, B., Pal, S., Pal, T. and Singh, S. P. (2019). "Green Smart Building: Requisites, Architecture, Challenges, and Use Cases," In Green Building Management and Smart Automation, A. Solanki and A. Nayyar, Eds., IGI Global.
3. Solanki, A., and Nayyar, A. (2019). Green Internet of Things (G-IoT): ICT Technologies, Principles, Applications, Projects, and Challenges. In Handbook of Research on Big Data and the IoT (pp. 379–405). IGI Global.
4. Batth, R. S., Nayyar, A., and Nagpal, A. (2018, August). Internet of Robotic Things: Driving Intelligent Robotics of Future-Concept, Architecture, Applications and Technologies. In 2018 4th International Conference on Computing Sciences (ICCS) (pp. 151–160). IEEE.
5. Sanders, A, Elangeswaran, C. and Wulfsberg, J. (2016). Industry 4.0 Implies Lean Manufacturing: Research Activities in Industry 4.0 Function as Enablers for Lean Manufacturing. J. Ind. Eng. Manag, 9(3).
6. Kaur, A., Gupta, P., Singh, M., and Nayyar, A. (2019). Data Placement in Era of Cloud Computing: a Survey, Taxonomy and Open Research Issues. Scalable Computing: Practice and Experience, 20 (2), 377–398.
7. Singh, P., Gupta, P., Jyoti, K., and Nayyar, A. (2019). Research on Auto-Scaling of Web Applications in Cloud: Survey, Trends and Future Directions. Scalable Computing: Practice and Experience, 20(2), 399–432.
8. Singh, S. P., Nayyar, A., Kaur, H., and Singla, A. (2019). Dynamic Task Scheduling Using Balanced VM Allocation Policy for Fog Computing Platforms. Scalable Computing: Practice and Experience, 20(2), 433–456.
9. Singh, S. P., Nayyar, A., Kumar, R., and Sharma, A. (2019). Fog Computing: From Architecture to Edge Computing and Big Data Processing. The Journal of Supercomputing, 75(4), 2070–2105.

10. Pramanik, P. K. D., Upadhyaya, B., Pal, S. and Pal, T. (2018). "Internet of Things, Smart Sensors, and Pervasive Systems: Enabling the Connected and Pervasive Health Care," In Healthcare Data Analytics and Management, N. Dey, A. Ashour, S. J. Fong and C. Bhatt, Eds., Academic Press, , pp. 1–58.

11. Nayyar, A., and Puri, V. (2017). Comprehensive Analysis & Performance Comparison of Clustering Algorithms for Big Data. Review of Computer Engineering Research, 4(2), 54–80.

12. Pramanik, P. K. D., Pal, S. and Choudhury, P. (2018). "Beyond Automation: The Cognitive IoT. Artificial Intelligence Brings Sense to the Internet of Things," In Cognitive Computing for Big Data Systems Over IoT: Frameworks, Tools and ApplicationA. K. Sangaiah, A. Thangavelu and V. M. Sundaram, Eds., Springer, , pp. 1–37.

13. Reality Technologies (2019). "The Ultimate Guide to Understanding Augmented Reality (AR) Technology," Reality Technologies [Online]. Available: https://www.realitytechnologies.com/aug mented-reality/. [Accessed 11 May 2019].

14. EOS GmbH (May 2018). "Additive Manufacturing, Laser-Sintering and industrial 3D printing - Benefits and Functional Principle," EOS GmbH. [Online]. Available: https://www.eos.info/additive_manufacturing/for_technology_interested. [Accessed 11 May 2019].

15. Raileanu, S., Borangiu, T., Morariu, O. and Iacob, I. (2018). "Edge Computing in Industrial IoT Framework for Cloud-based Manufacturing Control," In 22nd International Conference on System Theory, Control and Computing (ICSTCC).

16. Pontrandolfo, P. and Okogbaa, O. G. (1999). Global Manufacturing: A Review and a Framework for Planning in a Global Corporation. International Journal of Production Economics, 37(1), 1–19.

17. Bharath, V. G. and Pati, R. (2015). "Virtual Manufacturing: A Review," International Journal of Engineering Research & Technology, 355–364.

Chapter 3

Industry 4.0 Applications in the Healthcare Sector: The Dawn of Healthcare 4.0

Fathy Yassin Alkhatib, Juman Khaldoon Alsadi,
Mariam Ali Ramadan, Jiju Antony, and Vikas Swarnakar
Department of Management Science and Engineering, Khalifa University, Abu Dhabi

3.1 Introduction

Multiple important sectors are transforming continuously as we travel deeper into the digitalization and modern technologies era that was initiated by the Fourth Industrial Revolution (Industry 4.0). Therefore, the demand for more advanced, cost-effective, and efficient solutions rose significantly. A major beneficiary of that is the healthcare field. The deployment of state-of-the-art Industry 4.0 tools allowed for rapid advancements in the healthcare sector, and so, the term "Healthcare 4.0" was coined. Mark Wehde [1] referred to Healthcare 4.0 as the modern healthcare system that is more patient-oriented and virtual-based rather than clinic-based, through the heavy reliance on novel technologies such as artificial intelligence (AI), machine learning, deep learning, 3D printing, robotics, and data analytics. This book chapter discusses the role of Industry 4.0 in the field of healthcare and highlights the current deployment trends and challenges as seen in healthcare organizations. Furthermore, this chapter provides future research directions in Healthcare 4.0.

DOI: 10.4324/9781003439684-3

3.2 Research Methodology

The methodology followed is an exhaustive exploration of past and present published and unpublished research on a particular topic carried out through the use of a systematic literature review (SLR) [2]. The main objective of employing the SLR is to analyze existing research findings and identify the challenges present. The systematic literature review is conducted on selected journal papers from time period 2018 to 2022. The time period considered is only four years since Healthcare 4.0 has only recently gained insight. As Scopus includes other resources and allows browsing and filtering of papers [3,4], only the Scopus database is used to collect the data. The initial result of searching for papers was 196 without considering the period, language, and type of paper. As a result of adding the exclusion criteria, the number of papers decreased to 76. Papers are reviewed based on their abstracts to ensure they are relevant to the main objective, and 23 articles are considered. The methodological flow of SLR is portrayed in Figure 3.1.

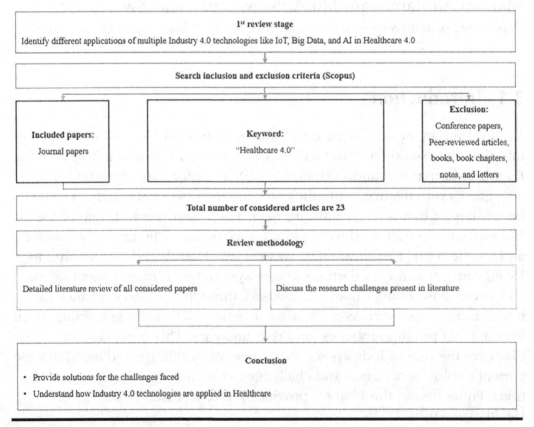

Figure 3.1   Methodological flow.

3.3 Literature Review

This chapter discusses the main applications and challenges of integrating Industry 4.0 and its applications in the healthcare sector. The first section highlights Industry 4.0 in the context of healthcare. The second section analyzes the main applications and challenges of using AI, whereas the third section spots the light on how IoT devices made it possible to collect copious amounts of valuable data and the big data techniques used to handle and analyze them.

3.3.1 *Industry 4.0 in Healthcare*

Healthcare institutions are moving toward eHealth or Healthcare 4.0, indicating that the industry is already experiencing the effects of Industry 4.0's rapid and severe technical progress [5]. As a result, various studies have investigated the feasibility of applying Industry 4.0 in the medical and healthcare sectors. A thorough review of the eHealth system is undertaken in one research paper [5], considering the impact of IoT technology, big data technology, and fog computing. The research examines how Industry 4.0 technologies are implemented in the healthcare sector. It depicts some of the most critical technologies to be deployed and the benefits, challenges, and issues related to their implementation.

Furthermore, since the state-of-the-art applications of Industry 4.0 technologies in healthcare have yet to be the subject of an extensive review, scholars and practitioners investigated to highlight the current research on the topic, significant gaps, and future research directions [6]. Additionally, an analysis of Healthcare 4.0 has been conducted [7] to identify any challenges, gaps, or tendencies. In [7], researchers discovered that Healthcare 4.0 deployments in hospital information management successfully used interdisciplinary approaches with various applications and functionalities. Therefore, the study was oriented toward practical application and academic alignment. Another study [2] focused mainly on Healthcare 4.0 and how it is attained from Industry 4.0. According to the authors, the Wisdom Pyramid Methodology was used to understand the broad range of technologies enabling Industry 4.0 and Healthcare 4.0 to provide more efficient, effective services. A systematic review of the digital technologies available in Healthcare 4.0 was conducted as part of the study.

3.3.2 AI in Healthcare 4.0

In the last 20 years, artificial intelligence (AI) has become increasingly prevalent in the healthcare sector, particularly with the advent of Healthcare 4.0, integrating AI, the Internet of Things (IoT), and big data analytics [2]. With artificial intelligence, healthcare quality can be enhanced, costs can be reduced, and efficiency can be increased via various applications [8]: AI can examine medical images to assist in the accurate and early diagnosis of diseases [9]. Moreover, AI can study large volumes of drug data to aid in the speedy development and assessment of drugs [10]. Another application of AI in Healthcare 4.0 constitutes patient monitoring: Medical professionals can monitor patients continuously with wearable devices and sensors based on artificial intelligence, permitting earlier intervention [2]. In [11], the authors discuss the role of artificial intelligence in precision medicine. A personalized medicine approach would use AI rather than developing treatments for populations and making medical decisions based on a few similar physical characteristics amongst patients. Another study sheds light on the use of AI in administrative tasks to facilitate the scheduling of appointments, billing, and insurance claims processing, improving the overall process accuracy and efficiency [12,13].

Nevertheless, AI faces numerous challenges in healthcare, including data acquisition, technology development, implementation, and social factors [14]. First, data accessibility is complicated due to the reluctance of numerous hospitals to share their data, as data is deemed a susceptible and regular target for breaches. Likewise, healthcare organizations are skeptical of adopting AI-based interventions considering the lack of empirical research on the effect of AI on patient outcomes. An imperishable worry regarding AI in healthcare is the possibility of human labor, promoting cynicism and opposition toward AI-based interventions. As to AI implementation, patient data may contain bias, inconsistencies, inaccuracies, and a lack of standardized format, making it hard for AI systems to conduct data analysis or make unbiased predictions.

3.3.3 IoT and Big Data in Healthcare 4.0

Technologies like IoT devices and big data analytics are widely utilized in several areas like automation of factories, smart cities, and different services. Healthcare is no exception, and it adopted these technologies later on. Modern IoT devices generate massive amounts of data, which makes data interpretation difficult [15]. To apply big data methods, data acquired by IoT devices must possess three key characteristics: volume, velocity, and variety. However, IoT devices struggle to handle massive amounts of data that must be processed at high speeds. Thus, these devices must be integrated with big data in order to facilitate data storage, processing, and analysis [16]. The role of IoT devices is to gather useful data, which is a raw task in nature. Therefore, IoT devices and big data are usually interconnected, with one collecting data and the other storing and analyzing it [17]. The utilization of IoT systems with big data enabled researchers to investigate many opportunities for IoT systems developments. Yet, new challenges will arise and must be overcome before this integration can reach its full potential [7,18,19].

Wireless body sensor networks (WBSNs) are one of the most important IoT applications in healthcare. It consists of several sensors deployed around the patient's body and allows doctors and nurses to monitor vital health parameters [20]. The sensors are deployed in a layer-based structure, where each layer is responsible for a specific task like sensing, communication, and storage [21]. In this way, IoT devices laid the groundwork for big data methods to shine by feeding them with the required amount of data. By the year 2025, [22] mentioned that over 25 billion devices will be connected to the IoT, where many of these are medical devices like blood sugar, pressure, heart rate, and body masses sensors. As a result, the volume of generated data will rise exponentially in the upcoming year. Big data methods are deployed to analyze the huge amount of data in short time intervals [23]. The usage of big data in healthcare systems is closely tied to five main processes: data acquisition, data storage, data, management, data analysis, and data visualization and report [24]. The techniques of big data can be widely applied to almost any modern management system. In healthcare, big data can be applied in five main areas: pharmaceuticals, organic and molecular applications, insurance and claim, design and manufacturing of devices, and personalized care [24]. Table 3.1 summarizes the applications of big data in healthcare and their respective areas.

Practitioners highlighted that managing large amounts of processed data is a major challenge in their organizations [25]. The data must be stored in a readable and accessible format. Machine learning and data mining techniques were created by experts from many fields to annotate and show the data in a suitable manner, allowing hospitals to easily process and analyze past medical records using big data in order to help patients predict and prevent multiple

Table 3.1 Summary of Big Data Applications and Areas in Healthcare

Application	Area
Assist in drug discovery and development, i.e., precision medicine analysis conducted by Pfizer [24].	Pharmaceutical
Understand strategies of illnesses and raise the precision of medical therapies.	Organic and molecular
Insurance claims management, scam detection, and underwriting.	Claim and Insurance
Develop material selection plans, investigate delivery approaches, and study tissue interactions.	Design and manufacturing of devices
Analyze patient's needs and requirements and create updated clinical guidelines to design modified healthcare program.	Personalized care

severe diseases [25,26]. Another issue emerges while dealing with such massive amounts of data, which is keeping medical records safe and secure from prospective hackers and data breaches. Researchers [19] mentioned that to safely secure healthcare data, IP addresses, geographical location, and constant key length encryption techniques are used. The function of IoT devices and big data in the healthcare industry is summarized in Figure 3.2.

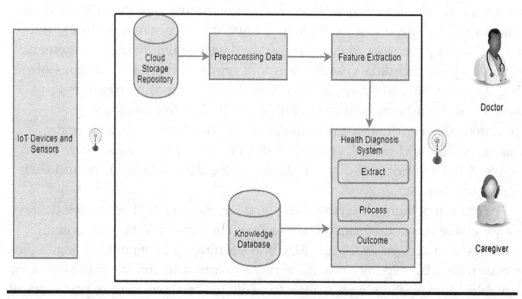

Figure 3.2   The role of IoT devices and big data in the healthcare industry. Courtesy of Rashid et al. (2021) [see 25].

3.4 Results and Discussions

Healthcare 4.0 stemmed from the transformative impact of leveraging Industry 4.0 technologies in the healthcare sector. These technologies foster enhanced operational performance, improved quality of patient care, and the overall efficaciousness of healthcare systems. For example, IoT sensors deployed around the patient's body allow prompt data processing and scrutinization of vital health parameters by tracking medication compliance. Likewise, big data can facilitate data acquisition, storage, management, analysis, and visualization. Moreover, big data can assist in diagnosis accuracy and drug development, analysis of patients' needs and requirements, and scam detection. In addition, AI-powered systems can recognize images and speech, process natural language, and perform predictive analytics to boost patient outcomes. By integrating these technologies, the healthcare industry can optimize resource utilization, diminish wait times, and enhance the patient experience by gathering and studying patient data in real time. In general, Healthcare 4.0 is creating the foundation for a more efficient, cost-effective, and patient-centered healthcare system by incorporating Industry 4.0 technologies.

Nonetheless, Industry 4.0 applications in Healthcare 4.0 introduces several challenges. A vital challenge constitutes the reluctance of healthcare providers to share patient data, fearing potential patient privacy and data security breaches. Likewise, acquiring information from several data sources, including wearables and IoT devices, may generate inconsistencies and inaccuracies in analyzing and interpreting patient data. In summary, while Industry 4.0 technologies present substantial advantages to healthcare, their deployment encompasses numerous challenges.

3.5 Conclusion, Limitations, and Direction for Future Research

This chapter discusses the applications of multiple Industry 4.0 technologies like the Internet of Things (IoT), big data, and artificial intelligence (AI) in Healthcare 4.0. A systematic literature review is conducted in order to identify several challenges faced in the healthcare sector. Also, it is used to determine the different Industry 4.0 technologies applied and implemented in several healthcare areas.

This chapter provides professionals, practitioners, and managers of organizations with a guide to understanding how Industry 4.0 is applied in different sectors and provides several solutions for significant challenges faced. This chapter identified several scientific gaps in the literature, as studies investigating the adoption of Industry 4.0 in the healthcare sector have yet to be found.

The limitations faced in this study are finding academic material to support the adoption of Industry 4.0 in the healthcare industry. Also, the majority of scholarly data is review studies; however, papers that discuss the implementation with tangible results are yet to be made available. For future research, a framework that is tested and validated could be initiated using the determined challenges. Also, analyzing the best Industry 4.0 technologies that have a significant impact on the healthcare sector must be determined through actual case studies.

References

1. Wehde, M. (2019). Healthcare 4.0. *IEEE Engineering Management Review*, *47*(3), 24–28.
2. Jayaraman, P. P., Forkan, A. R. M., Morshed, A., Haghighi, P. D., & Kang, Y. B. (2020). Healthcare 4.0: A review of frontiers in digital health. *Wiley Interdisciplinary Reviews: Data Mining and Knowledge Discovery, 10*(2), e1350.
3. Koemtzi, M. D., Psomas, E., Antony, J., & Tortorella, G. L. (2022). Lean manufacturing and human resources: A systematic literature review on future research suggestions. *Total Quality Management & Business Excellence*, 1–28.
4. da Silva, F. F., Filser, L. D., Juliani, F., & de Oliveira, O. J. (2018). Where to direct research in lean six sigma?: Bibliometric analysis, scientific gaps and trends on literature. *International Journal of Lean Six Sigma, 9*(3). 10.1108/IJLSS-05-2017-0052.
5. Aceto, G., Persico, V., & Pescapé, A. (2020). Industry 4.0 and health: Internet of things, big data, and cloud computing for healthcare 4.0. *Journal of Industrial Information Integration, 18*, 100129.
6. Liao, Y., Deschamps, F., Loures, E. D. F. R., & Ramos, L. F. P. (2017). Past, present and future of Industry 4.0–A systematic literature review and research agenda proposal. *International Journal of Production Research, 55*(12), 3609–3629.
7. Tortorella, G. L., Fogliatto, F. S., Mac Cawley Vergara, A., Vassolo, R., & Sawhney, R. (2020). Healthcare 4.0: Trends, challenges and research directions. *Production Planning & Control, 31*(15), 1245–1260.
8. Vinodh, S., Antony, J., Agrawal, R., & Douglas, J. A. (2021). Integration of continuous improvement strategies with Industry 4.0: A systematic review and agenda for further research. *The TQM Journal, 33*(2), 441–472.

9. Kishor, A., & Chakraborty, C. (2022). Artificial intelligence and Internet of Things based healthcare 4.0 monitoring system. *Wireless Personal Communications, 127*(2), 1615–1631.
10. Milne-Ives, M., de Cock, C., Lim, E., Shehadeh, M. H., de Pennington, N., Mole, G., … & Meinert, E. (2020). The effectiveness of artificial intelligence conversational agents in health care: Systematic review. *Journal of Medical Internet Research, 22*(10), e20346.
11. Raja, R., Kumar, S., Rani, S., & Laxmi, K. R. (Eds.). (2020). *Artificial intelligence and machine learning in 2D/3D medical image processing.* CRC Press.
12. Alqahtani, A. (2022). Application of artificial intelligence in discovery and development of anticancer and antidiabetic therapeutic agents. *Evidence-Based Complementary and Alternative Medicine, 2022.*
13. Davenport, T., & Kalakota, R. (2019). The potential for artificial intelligence in healthcare. *Future Healthcare Journal, 6*(2), 94.
14. Vetter, N. (2021). The promise of artificial intelligence: A review of the opportunities and challenges of artificial intelligence in healthcare and clinical trials in skeletal dysplasia: A paradigm for treating rare diseases. *British Medical Bulletin, 139*(1), 1–3.
15. Dehkordi, S. A., Farajzadeh, K., Rezazadeh, J., Farahbakhsh, R., Sandrasegaran, K., & Dehkordi, M. A. (2020). A survey on data aggregation techniques in IoT sensor networks. *Wireless Networks, 26*(2), 1243–1263.
16. Chen, Z., Chen, S., & Feng, X. (2016). A design of distributed storage and processing system for internet of vehicles. In *2016 8th International Conference on Wireless Communications & Signal Processing (WCSP)* (pp. 1e5). IEEE.
17. Ahmed, E., Yaqoob, I., Hashem, I. A. T., Khan, I., Ahmed, A. I. A., Imran, M., et al. (2017). The role of big data analytics in Internet of Things. *Computer Networks, 129,* 459e471.
18. Rashid, M., Singh, H., & Goyal, V. (2019). Cloud storage privacy in health care systems based on IP and geo-location validation using K-mean clustering technique. *International Journal of E-Health and Medical Communications, 10*(4), 54e65.
19. Rashid, M., Hamid, A., & Parah, S. A. (2019). Analysis of streaming data using big data and hybrid machine learning approach. In A. Singh, & A. Mohan (Eds.), *Handbook of Multimedia Information Security: Techniques and Applications.* Springer.
20. Alkhayyat, A., Thabit, A. A., Al-Mayali, F. A., & Abbasi, Q. H. (2019). WBSN in IoT health-based application: toward delay and energy consumption minimization. *Journal of Sensors, Hindawi, 2508452,* 14.
21. Li, W., Chai, Y., Khan, F., Jan, S. R. U., Verma, S., Menon, V. G., & Li, X. (2021). A comprehensive survey on machine learning-based big data analytics for IoT-enabled smart healthcare system. *Mobile Networks and Applications, 26,* 234–252.
22. Gartner. (2014). Gartner says the Internet of Things will transform the data center. Available from http://www.gartner.com/newsroom/id/2684616.

23. Dey, N., Hassanien, A. E., Bhatt, C., Ashour, A. S., & Satapathy, S. C. (Eds.). (2018). *Internet of things and big data analytics toward next-generation intelligence.* Springer.
24. Senthilkumar, S. A., Rai, B. K., Meshram, A. A., Gunasekaran, A., & Chandrakumarmangalam, S. (2018). Big data in healthcare management: A review of literature. *American Journal of Theoretical and Applied Business,* 4(2), 57–69.
25. Rashid, M., Singh, H., Goyal, V., Parah, S. A., & Wani, A. R. (2021). Big data based hybrid machine learning model for improving performance of medical Internet of Things data in healthcare systems. In *Healthcare Paradigms in the Internet of Things Ecosystem* (pp. 47–62). Academic Press.
26. Dash, S., Shakyawar, S. K., Sharma, M., & Kaushik, S. (2019). Big data in healthcare: Management, analysis and future prospects. *Journal of Big Data,* 6(1), 1–25.

Chapter 4

Role of Industry 4.0 for Sustainable Future in Power Industries

Shashi Kant Verma

National Institute of Technology Durgapur, West Bengal, India

4.1 Introduction

The Industrial Revolution 4.0 helps engineers, researchers, and scientists to deliver real value. Digital technologies such as machine learning, artificial intelligence, deep learning, and the Internet of Things (IoT) not only enhance productivity but also increase thermal efficiency in the next-generation energy sector. Paramount amidst an organization's most treasured assets are its data. All such technologies leverage the internet and such high computing infrastructure to connect people, machines, material, money, and time. These technologies help in increased flexibility and optimizing decision making. As technology continues to progress, we can believe to see even more growth in this area in the coming years.

This chapter mainly focuses on the recent work based on Industry 4.0 on various types of the power plant. The discussion of some of the good works based on the Industry 4.0 technologies in power plants and their overall impact on energy production is presented. Some of the mathematical models are also discussed, which are applied for error quantification involved in predicted models.

DOI: 10.4324/9781003439684-4

4.2 Recent Works Based on Industry 4.0 in Energy Sector

This review comprises a global investigation of different predictive tools involved in Industry 4.0 along with their findings. Table 2.1 shows the recent work on the use of digital technologies in various energy sectors. From Table 4.1, it is clear that Industry 4.0 is not only involved in coal-based power plants but also in solar, hydro, wind, and nuclear power plants. Applying digital technologies for decision making and optimization of transmission lines in the hydropower plant predicted maximum bubble diameter, and maximum cladding temperature of nuclear fuel bundle can further enhance smart power generation operations.

Table 4.1 Recent work by use of digital technologies in various energy sectors

Researchers	Applied AI techniques	Remarks
Krzywanski et al. [1]	Artificial Neural Network (ANN)	ANN is a powerful reliable technique for decision making and data analysis in coal-based thermal power plants.
Natgunanathan et al. [2]	Prediction models based on machine learning (ML)	The ANN-based prediction model is highly efficient for solar power generation.
Kumar et al. [3]	ANN	The curve-fitting model is less efficient than the ANN model for the forecasted power generated.
Kumar and Saini [4]	Internet of Things based cloud computing	The system can be used for reaction turbine-based hydropower plants.
Ahmed et al. [5]	Genetic Algorithm (GA)-Traveling Salesman Problem Method (TSPM) and Fuzzy GA-TSP	Comparison of two approaches for optimization of the transmission line.
Sleiti et al. [6]	Anomaly detection and deep Learning (ADL)	They have discussed key challenges associated with digital twins in the energy sector.
Dong et al. [7]	ANN	They predicted the maximum bubble diameter by using ANN.

(continued)

Table 4.1 *(Continued)* **Recent work by use of digital technologies in various energy sectors**

Researchers	Applied AI techniques	Remarks
Sallehhudin and Diab [8]	ML	They have applied ML to predict maximum cladding temperature. And concluded that it is a decision-making tool under accident conditions.
Hossain et al. [9]	The deep learning-based hybrid model	The deep learning-based hybrid model performed better than other forecasting methods.
Zhou and Tan [10]	NN	They have broadly discussed the neural network-based approach to nuclear power plant control.

4.3 Performance Evaluation of Applied Predictive Model

Industry 4.0 plays an important role by using emerging technologies such as the Internet of Things (IoT), robotics, and AI to increase productivity, enhance safety, and quality control of the end product. Figure 4.1 shows the Fourth Industrial Revolution in the context of the coal-based power plant. The sensors are used in all types of the power plant. And a huge amount of data is constantly collected and stored. These data could be used for decision making and optimization. The data are logged during the testing and

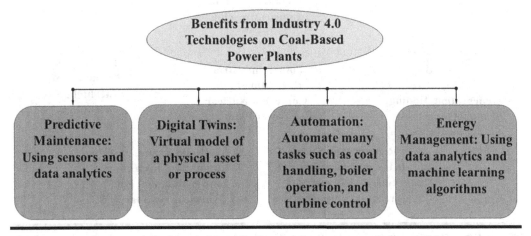

Figure 4.1 The Fourth Industrial Revolution in the context of the coal-based power plant.

commissioning of newly fabricated machines during research and development activities. These data can be used for optimization by using an AI algorithm. Krzywinski et al. [1] applied Industry 4.0 to the supercritical power plant for the optimization of performance. They calculate mean absolute percentage error and root-mean-square error for the evaluation of the developed AI model. Equation 4.1 represents the mean absolute error as a function of sample size (N), real values (Y_i) and forecasted values ($\widehat{Y_i}$).

$$\textit{Mean absolute error } (\%) = \frac{1}{N} \sum_{i=1}^{N} \left| \frac{\hat{Y_i} - Y_i}{Y_i} \right| * 100\% \qquad (4.1)$$

$$\textit{Root mean square error} = \left(\frac{1}{N} \sum_{i=1}^{N} (\hat{Y_i} - Y_i)^2 \right)^{\frac{1}{2}} \qquad (4.2)$$

Industry 4.0, through the digitalization of power plant processes, can offer prospects to advance energy production systems. Figure 4.2 shows the Fourth Industrial Revolution in the context of the nuclear power plant. Predictive maintenance is a precarious feature of Industry 4.0 in the power sector. By using sensors and data analytics, firms can predict when equipment will need maintenance. This concept will be reducing downtime and improve the efficiency of machines and devices.

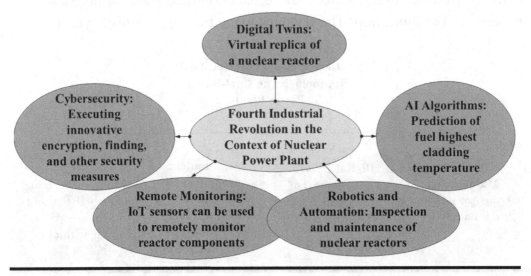

Figure 4.2   The Fourth Industrial Revolution in the context of the nuclear power plant.

Figure 4.3 shows the Fourth Industrial Revolution in the context of the wind power plant. The robots can be used in that area of the turbine section, where it is difficult to reach or is not accessible. Different types of sensors can be used to monitor power output, wind speed, and wind temperature. Figure 4.4 shows the AI application in a hydropower plant.

The sensors are used to quantify the water level and flow rate of rivers, which can be examined to forecast future water availability. This information

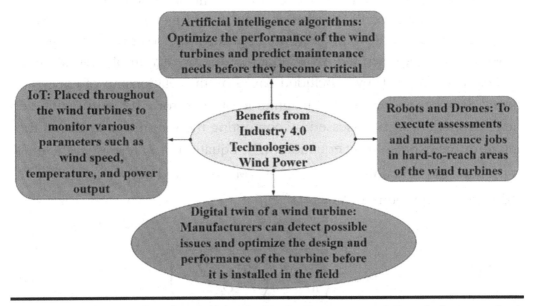

Figure 4.3   The Fourth Industrial Revolution in the context of the wind power plant.

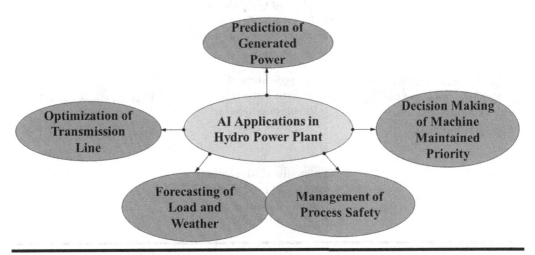

Figure 4.4   AI application in hydropower plant.

can then be used to optimize the use of the hydropower plant at maximum overall efficiency. The weather data are collected by using Industry 4.0 technologies, including satellite images and weather sensors. Then collected data could be analyzed and enhanced by the optimization of the forecasted weather.

Bryden et al. [11] have developed a methodology to detect an irregular operation of the gas turbine cycle by online technique. Sozen et al. [12] have used an optimization technique based on an artificial neural network to predict the thermodynamic properties of R508B refrigerant. Figure 4.5 shows the Fourth Industrial Revolution in the context of the solar power plant.

Sen et al. [13] applied the ANN model for the prediction of heat rate from the heat exchanger. They concluded based on the relationship of experimental data sets and calculated magnitude of the error. The performance of the ANN model can be assessed by computing the root-mean square of the output errors expressed by equation (4.3). Equation (4.2) represent the error as the function of training numbers sets (M), predicted output values (O_i^{Pre}), and experimental output values (O_i^{exp}).

$$E_{rms} = \sqrt{\frac{1}{M}\sum_{i=1}^{M}\left(\frac{O_i^{Pre} - O_i^{exp}}{O_i^{exp}}\right)^2} \qquad (4.3)$$

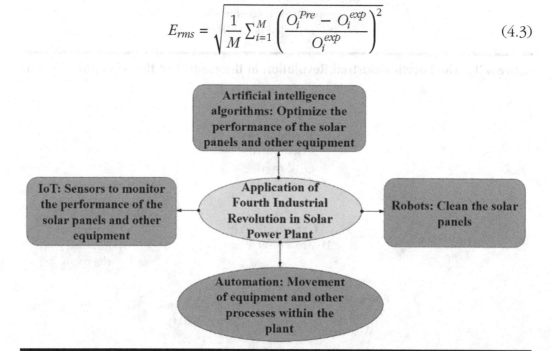

Figure 4.5   The Fourth Industrial Revolution in the context of the solar power plant.

Recently, Lima et al. [14] have applied Industry 4.0 in the university campus for power plant control and concluded that such correlation can be applied to other types of power plants. Interested readers should go through the paper for more details related to the predictive model of sub-critical coal-based power plant. The schedule of maintenance plays a vital role in any type of industry to avoid unplanned breakdowns. The modern power plant has a lot of complexity which calls for optimization of maintenance for sensors-enabled technology. In this context, Baraldi et al. [15] have discussed the different types of optimization techniques in Industry 4.0. They concluded that ML and AI algorithms offer an important role to predict present and future health conditions of plant components. Deng et al. [16] have given a broad review on AI application to nuclear reactors. They have tabulated the different applications of AI along with prediction models for the nuclear reactor.

4.4 Challenges

The challenges associated with the implementation of Industry 4.0 in power plants mainly involve data management and cybersecurity. The adoption of Industry 4.0 requires specialized skilled manpower and knowledge. The smart power plant would work smartly when the manpower and machines will be up to date with digital transformation tools. The data should be properly managed with the incorporation of all safety measures within the plant. Figure 4.6 depicts the challenges allied with the Fourth Industrial

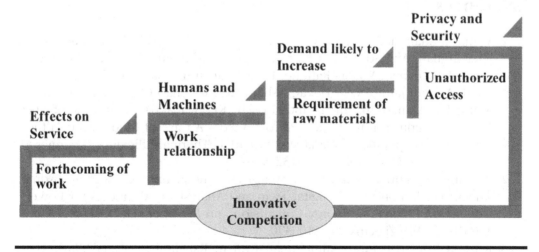

Figure 4.6   Challenges allied with the Fourth Industrial Revolution in the context of the energy sector.

Revolution in the context of the energy sector. The proper utilization of manpower and machine is also one of the challenges in the smart factory. New technology like robotics and IoT computerize the task in the power plant as well as help ease our routine work. There must be a protocol set globally to use Industry 4.0 so that the emerging technology can balance the impact of society and the workforce.

4.5 Recommendations and Conclusion

The Fourth Industrial Revolution and digital twins are becoming obligatory necessities in the energy sector to improve productivity and enhance safety. By adopting Fourth Industrial Revolution–based technologies, operators can reduce costs, improve performance, and contribute to a smart energy future. For the hazardous area, AI-based techniques are one of the emerging techniques to predict the performance of machines. AI-based techniques can be utilized to predict the thermo-physical properties of the fluid, which minimize efforts and computational time. In the two-phase flow analysis, the ANN model plays a vital role in the prediction of the maximum diameter of the bubble. Overall, the integration of Industry 4.0 technologies can help to improve the efficiency and reliability of different types of power plants, leading to cost savings and a more sustainable energy supply.

References

1. Waqar Muhammad Ashraf, Ghulam Moeen Uddin, Syed Muhammad Arafat, Sher Afghan, Ahmad Hassan Kamal, Muhammad Asim, Muhammad Haider Khan, Muhammad Waqas Rafique, Uwe Naumann, Sajawal Gul Niazi, Hanan Jamil, Ahsaan Jamil, Nasir Hayat, Ashfaq Ahmad, Shao Changkai, Liu Bin Xiang, Ijaz Ahmad Chaudhary and Jaroslaw Krzywanski, Optimization of a 660 MWe Supercritical Power Plant Performance – A Case of Industry 4.0 in the Data-Driven Operational Management Part 1. Thermal Efficiency, Energies 13(21) (2020), 5592; 10.3390/en13215592.
2. Iynkaran Natgunanathan, Vicky Mak-Hau, Sutharshan Rajasegarar, Adnan Anwar, Deakin Microgrid Digital Twin and Analysis of AI Models for Power Generation Prediction, Energy Conversion and Management: X 18 (2023) 100370; 10.1016/j.ecmx.2023.100370.
3. Krishna Kumar, Gaurav Saini, Aman Kumar, Rajvikram Madurai Elavarasan, Zafar Said, Vladimir Terzija, Effective Monitoring of Pelton Turbine Based

Hydropower Plants Using Data-Driven Approach, Electrical Power and Energy Systems 149 (2023) 109047; 10.1016/j.ijepes.2023.109047.

4. Krishna Kumar, and R.P. Saini, Data-Driven Internet of Things and Cloud Computing Enabled Hydropower Plant Monitoring System, Sustainable Computing: Informatics and Systems 36 (2022) 100823; 10.1016/j.suscom.2022.100823.

5. F. Chen Jong, Musse Mohamud Ahmed, W. Kin Lau, and H. Aik Denis Lee, A New Hybrid Artificial Intelligence (AI) Approach for Hydro Energy Sites Selection and Integration, Heliyon 8 (2022) e10638; 10.1016/j.heliyon.2022.e10638.

6. Ahmad K. Sleiti, Jayanta S. Kapat, and Ladislav Vesely, Digital Twin in Energy Industry: Proposed Robust Digital Twin for Power Plant and Other Complex Capital-Intensive Large Engineering Systems, Energy Reports 8 (2022) 3704–3726; 10.1016/j.egyr.2022.02.305.

7. Xiaomeng Dong, Haoxian Chen, Changwei Li, Ming Yang, Yang Yu and Xi Huang, An Evaluation of the Data-Driven Model for Bubble Maximum Diameter in Subcooled Boiling Flow Using Artificial Neural Networks, Frontiers in Energy Research, 15 (August 2022), Sec. Nuclear Energy; Volume 10 – 2022; 10.3389/fenrg.2022.903464.

8. Wazif Sallehhudin and Aya Diab, Using Machine Learning to Predict the Fuel Peak Cladding Temperature for a Large Break Loss of Coolant Accident, Frontiers in Energy Research, 08 (October 2021), Sec. Nuclear Energy; Volume 9 – 2021; 10.3389/fenrg.2021.755638.

9. Md Alamgir Hossain, Ripon K. Chakrabortty, Sondoss Elsawah, and Michael J. Ryan, Very Short-Term Forecasting of Wind Power Generation Using Hybrid Deep Learning Model, Journal of Cleaner Production 296 (2021) 126564; 10.1016/j.jclepro.2021.126564.

10. Gang Zhou and Da Tan, Review of Nuclear Power Plant Control Research: Neural Network-Based Methods, Annals of Nuclear Energy 181 (2023) 109513; 10.1016/j.anucene.2022.109513.

11. Bonilla-Alvarado, Bryden, Shadle, Tucker, and Pezzini, Development of Real-Time System Identification to Detect Abnormal Operations in a Gas Turbine Cycle, Journal of Energy Resources Technology 142 (2020) 1–40, 10.1115/1.4046144.

12. Adnan Sozen, Mehmet Ozalp, and Erol Arcaklioglu, Calculation for the Thermodynamic Properties of an Alternative Refrigerant (R508B) Using Artificial Neural Network, Applied Thermal Engineering 27 (2007) 551–559; http://dx.doi.org/10.1016/j.applthermaleng.2006.06.003.

13. Arturo Pacheco-Vega, Mihir Sen, K.T. Yang, and Rodney L. McClain, Neural Network Analysis of Fin-Tube Refrigerating Heat Exchanger with Limited Experimental Data, International Journal of Heat and Mass Transfer 44 (2001) 763–770; 10.1016/S0017-9310(00)00139-3.

14. Daniel Kestering, Selorme Agbleze, Heleno Bispo, and Fernando V. Lima, Model Predictive Control of Power Plant Cycling Using Industry 4.0

Infrastructure, Digital Chemical Engineering 7 (2023) 100090; 10.1016/j.dche.2023.100090.

15. Luca Pinciroli, Piero Baraldi, Enrico Zio, Maintenance Optimization in Industry 4.0, Reliability Engineering and System Safety 234 (2023) 109204; 10.1016/j.ress.2023.109204.

16. Qingyu Huang, Shinian Peng, Jian Deng, Hui Zeng, Zhuo Zhang, Yu Liu, and Peng Yuan, A Review of the Application of Artificial Intelligence to Nuclear Reactors, Where We Are and What's Next, Heliyon 9 (2023) e13883; 10.1016/j.heliyon.2023.e13883.

Chapter 5

Industry 4.0 and Its Role in a Sustainable Supply Chain for Green Manufacturing

Chandra Prakash Dewangan, Ajay Tripathi, and Govind Sahu
Department of Mechanical Engineering, Government Engineering College Raipur, Chhattisgarh, India

5.1 Introduction

Resources and population are two important issues nowadays. The environment is very significant, and any change in the climate makes the earth's ecosystem unbalanced. The fundamental goal of this time is to reduce the harm that companies are doing to the environment. The price of goods and energy is constantly rising because of increasing demand and shortage of supply.[1] Because cost fluctuations are unpredictable, businesses attempt to produce successfully within wide energy and resource cost ranges. One way to adapt to pricing fluctuations is to pass markups forward to the customer. A price increase, however, can call for product improvements. Instead, improving the rate of production that can be accomplished by minimizing consumption and simplifying the industrial system could aid in maintaining constant costs.[2] The main aim of this chapter is to highlight the manufacturer of the goods, who is mass producing it. We've observed that a huge amount of energy is utilized every day, and plenty of waste is produced as well. These wastes are harmful and can bring about the end of humanity.

DOI: 10.4324/9781003439684-5

This chapter outlines every waste product as well as the green manufacturing techniques we can utilize to cut down on wastage and boost the usage of renewable energy. Implementing green manufacturing practices is frequently profitable as well as beneficial to the environment. Environmental effects are now seen as strategically important for corporate operations with the goal of lowering costs and producing high-quality goods.[3] Green operations (GOs) aims to save costs related to manufacturing. As per the literature on environmental studies, GO is focused on environmental practices that are both process- and product-oriented. Help decrease the impact that products and supply chain activities bring to natural resources.[3,4] Prior research on GOs has only concentrated on identifying the antecedents and how these influence implementation, such as institutional constraints, rules, and customer expectations. Implementing GO has both business and environmental benefits.[5,6] There is a widespread perception that organizations can successfully implement environmental policies and conduct sustainable business. Without this the performance outcomes of GO may be jeopardized. Green manufacturing can result in a shorter product life cycle, which lowers the product's cost. The ideal materials management system is created to recognize the relevance of the associated strategic variables and discover the impact of cost factors in a supply chain that is quite close to being green.[7] The "Industry 4.0" manufacturing innovation's revolutionary goal is to combine the real and virtual worlds. The most significant challenge is the seamless transition of current management and manufacturing processes to Industry 4.0 standards. In this area, there is still a ton of research to be done. It is necessary to improve infrastructure and skills. With the convergence of artificial intelligence, robotics, 3D printing, cloud computing, and Industrial Internet of Things, Industry 4.0 has a lot to offer in terms of realizing the vision of advanced factories, production, and commodities.[8,9]

5.2 Green Manufacturing (GM)

Green manufacturing is the process of incorporating eco-friendly production techniques into operations and using renewable resources to create products. Using less natural resources and environmental contaminants is a pledge made by green manufacturers. Additionally, green facilities strive to produce as little waste, carbon emissions, and environmental effects as they can.[10]

The idea of "green manufacturing" has been around since the 1990s,[11] but in the last few years, researchers have paid more attention to it as a result of pressure from various stakeholders on sustainability-related issues. The definition of green manufacturing is still up for debate among scholars, despite its widespread acceptance. To reduce waste and increase production, we define GM as the taking on quick, dependable, and energy-saving manufacturing processes and equipments. GM is also seen as uncommonly efficient production methods and manufacturing processes that use inputs that produce less to zero pollution and no wastage. This remarkably lessens the adverse environmental impact.[12,13]

5.2.1 Objective of Green Manufacturing

It refers to the production of goods using environmentally friendly methods. This includes switching from items that will run out, like oil, to sustainable resources like solar and wind energy. Consumers are starting to favor manufacturers who use eco-friendly practices, which are being adopted by many of them. Companies that care about the environment are preferred by customers and businesses. Being a green manufacturing firm means aiming to reduce the quantity of natural resources used, waste, pollution, and hazardous gas emissions during production by recycling and reusing materials.[14]

5.2.2 Transformation to Green Manufacturing

By concentrating on the following three areas, manufacturing organizations can overcome these issues:

1. **Green energy:** producing and utilizing cleaner energy. This is the initial step to take because industry depends on energy. Utilizing nonconventional energy sources, such as CNG, wind, solar, and biomass, as well as improving operational energy efficiency, are all included in "green energy."
2. **Green products:** making greener products. When describing green products, the terms "reuse," "low carbon footprint," "biological," and "eco-friendly" are frequently employed. Making green items may frequently cost more money. However, companies can increase sales and raise prices to offset the expense of manufacturing and marketing products that people want that are green.
3. **Green business operations procedures:** implementing green business operations processes. This necessitates systematic use of limited

resources, reduction of waste production through efficient operations, a smaller carbon footprint, and water conservation. Green business practices boost output and reduce expenses.[15]

5.2.3 Structure for Green Manufacturing Adoption

5.2.3.1 Obstacles in Acquiring Green

The commercial case for "green" is still strong even under challenging market conditions. There is a growing knowledge of the necessity of going green, as well as the necessity of addressing green in these areas: green processes, green goods, and green energy. However, businesses confront difficulties on a number of fronts, with establishing leadership for such an effort being the greatest difficulty.[16] Companies need to make the following transitions from: (a) a narrow focus on isolated, infrequently small-scale green projects to a more comprehensive strategy; (b) guaranteeing regulatory compliance to producing an environmental benefit; and (c) initiatives from being viewed as cost centers to being viewed as business possibilities. It necessitates a significant shift that, in order to be effective, demands a framework that addresses the three main obstacles to taking decisive action:

1. Businesses lack a thorough understanding of the factors and concerns that are important to them and their sectors, as well as what sustainability means to them.
2. It can be challenging for businesses to model a business case for sustainability, let alone come up with one that is convincing. Most people do not prioritize these activities, and since costs and technologies are still developing, it is frequently difficult to understand the economics.
3. Even companies that make use of green initiatives still do these duties in addition to their core business functions without incorporating them into their corporate strategies. Because of this, they are unable to reap the full benefits and the execution is poor.

5.2.3.2 Economic Analysis and Strategic Decision Making

Acquiring a greener lifestyle needs businesses to fully comprehend the costs, advantages, and range of green initiatives at their disposal. Making an economic assessment is just a small portion of the narrative. After presenting a convincing argument, businesses must decide to be strategically green. The selection of starting may fluctuate depending on the market environment and prospects for strategic differentiation, in addition to the underlying economics of the options. Potentially, businesses have the option of being the following:

A firm has the option of becoming "planet indifferent," which would entail adopting few environmental protection measures. "Green innovators," who strive to remain toward the front of the sustainability curve and shift the emphasis from risk management to top line growth and competitive advantage, or "good citizens," who implement a few isolated initiatives and go above and beyond what customers or regulators require.[17]

In contrast to the third choice, which commits the business to a thorough green strategy and to making the most of the efforts, the first two options do not allow the company to fully harness the potential of the green and are only relevant with a short-term lens.

5.2.3.3 Implementation Framework

The path to being green is one of extensive change. The preparation and execution of the initiatives must receive sufficient attention if they are to be successful. Early victories and triumphs are crucial for creating momentum. It necessitates a top management team that is totally dedicated, stringent periodic reviews, and ongoing internal and external communication. Green energy, green products, and green processes may all be put into practice utilizing a simple three-step methodology. Refer to Figure 5.1.

1. **Planning:** For instance, businesses must make a thorough plan to utilize more green energy, change their product line to greener options, and restructure their operations to adopt greener procedures. A sustainability charter that is built on both short- and long-term goals must include green goals. Businesses should create green indices that measure the results of the green policies they have implemented, set specific goals for the indices, and monitor their progress toward those goals.
2. **Implementation:** Being environmentally friendly should be incorporated into every step of the value chain, with a solid plan in place, measurable goals, and integration into the core business.
   * **Green energy:** Industries that manufacture goods that use a lot of energy must convert to greener energy sources and develop plans for using it more efficiently. Lowering the energy intensity of activities can be accomplished by the installation of captive wind or

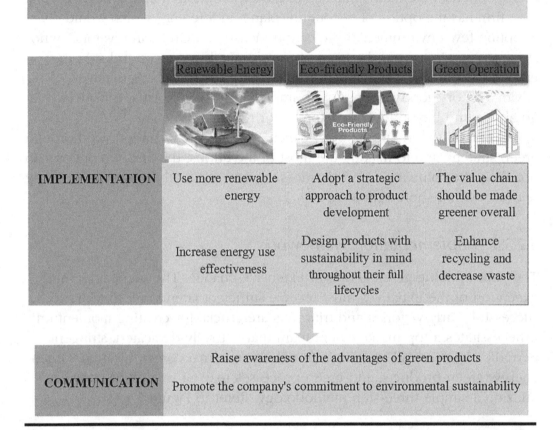

Figure 5.1   Structure for companies to successfully implement green technology.

solar power generation systems as well as energy-saving techniques like adopting LED lighting or better utilizing daylight in building design.

- **Green products:** Organizations should evaluate their offers based on three criteria in order to migrate to a portfolio of green products: How environmentally friendly the product is over the duration of its life cycle, the resources and energy consumed, and the production process are all factors. These factors can be quantified by businesses to evaluate the environmental value of their product offerings. Businesses should set goals for this measure during the planning phase and monitor their development over time.

- **Green business operations:** Companies must gradually rethink the operational processes used across the whole value chain. Changing to more environmentally friendly manufacturing techniques, making adjustments to cut waste, enhancing recycling, and motivating all sellers and buyers to take common activities are some examples of how to accomplish this.
3. **Communication:** For green programs to completely realize their potential benefits, a well-designed promotion strategy is just as crucial as thoughtful execution. Campaigns to educate customers about the company's green product options and its energy and operational practices can result in higher sales.[18,19]

5.3 Supply Chain Management (SCM)

The procedure of scheduling, applying, and continuously monitoring the supply chain in order to maximize efficiency is termed as supply chain management. SCM includes the control of final goods from start to consumption. The traditional supply chain consists of many businesses that make it possible for customers and suppliers to interact.[20]

The right amount of goods and services are produced and distributed to customers at the right time and place, all while meeting their service level requirements. SCM integrates vendors, goods producers, warehouses, and stores to eliminate the system-wide price. In order to deliver materials, information, components, and finished goods from starting to last consumers at a minimum cost per unit and with top-notch assistance, SCM is concentrated on integrating its logistics, procurement, process, and advertising functions with those of other supply chain participants.[21] Figure 5.2 explains the supply chain.

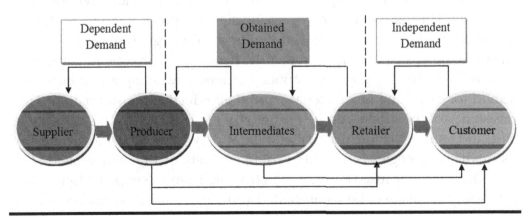

Figure 5.2   Supply chain management networking.

5.3.1 Green Supply Chain (GSC)

The use of environmental ethics and consideration of each typical SC system instance are referred to as "green supply chain" practices. Aim of the GSC is to eliminate unintentional pollution from each component and agent in the normal SC circuit, including dangerous biological particles, fossil fuels, hazardous particles, harmful particles, poisonous gases, etc. The green supply chain, which is utilized to gather, transform, and deliver raw resources to consumers, involves contractors, industrial facilities, warehouses, distribution centers, and sellers.[22]

When the Supply chain (SC) revolution began in 1990, managers in various industries paid attention to quantity and quality on their own but did not consider how their companies' SC actions and activities related to environmental (green) challenges. Green supply chains address the relationship between the purchasing function and measures such as material reduction, recycling, reprocessing, and replacement within the boundaries of the GSC, the standard SC network.[8]

5.3.2 Sustainability and Supply Chain

A supply chain is always required in order to deliver the value of a given company plan. The input is changed via a supply chain into a more valuable product. The sustainable supply chain idea is discussed in this section. Many gave Holweg's process model some thought.[23] A feedback loop was considered for repair, reverse logistics, recovery, refurbishing, and recycling. Regularity, acceptability, and productivity are the three primary production techniques that are related to the model in order to give it sustainability qualities. Additionally, the connection between the process model and the environment allows for a supply chain that is integrated with environmental concerns.[13] This has been done by connecting the process model to the framework for producing waste and the input of energy, water, and other renewable processes in order to repair the health of environment. Sufficiency is attained by the minimizing of inputs, efficiency by taking an appropriate method for extracting raw materials, and their effective transformation. The consistency of the model can be ensured by the feedback loop's capacity to reuse and reintroduce the material into the supply chain. The effectiveness of sustainability strategies is measured using a variety of valuation-related methodologies. Because of this, it is noticeable from the explanation earlier that supply chains may be incorporated with sustainability goals, and the impact can be measured by looking at the products' potential to affect the environment.[24]

5.4 Industry 4.0 (I 4.0)

Manufacturing has undergone a cyber-physical change, or "Industry 4.0," in the last 20 years. The phrase "Industrie 4.0" refers to a government project in Germany that promotes networked production and a digital combination of business, industries, and other operations.[25]

The First Industrial Revolution started at the end of the eighteenth century, and it was distinguished by the mechanism made possible by steam and water energy. Electricity had a key role in the Second Industrial Revolution, which have taken place at the starting of the twentieth century and was marked by mass production, assembly lines, and labor divisions. The third happened sometime in the early 1970s as a result of the increased automation of equipment and production procedures thanks to computers. The best way to explain the Fourth Industrial Revolution is as a continuation of the third.[26] Industry 4.0 focuses on interconnecting those computers, as opposed to ladder of Industry 3.0 which incorporated computers into the industrial process. Industry 4.0 goes much further than just enabling communication between devices on the manufacturing floor.

5.4.1 Industry 4.0 and Its Applications

The scientific community has recognized opportunities for the adoption of sustainable manufacturing approaches. Some of the potential found includes ways to use data to create viable business models and a structure for product life cycles with assessment loops. However, the opportunities that were found did not result in measurable advantages, which led to the future inspection plan. Though it is acknowledged that I 4.0 can aid in the development of sustainable business models, it is currently not apparent how this might be done. The information can be gathered from a variety of sources, including customers and raw materials.[27] However, the promise of value creation cannot be completely achieved until and until the obtained data is utilized. There are still gaps in the translation of the sustainable strategy-focused business model. Gap is still working to create a system that would enable the creation of sustainable products utilizing the information gathered about a product's life cycle. Although implementing an I 4.0

environment leads to greater quality products, made to order, and quicker and more efficient productive manufacturing systems, I 4.0 has not specifically addressed the sustainability challenges encountered by manufacturers. When sustainable innovation generates economic gains, sustainability is frequently addressed subtly. For instance, it does not necessarily imply that a company has become more sustainable if its revenue from the sale of the product remains constant while it enhances the revenue from the provision of services.[28]

5.4.2 Relation of I 4.0 with Sustainable Supply Chain

The client base becomes physically and digitally connected to the product as a result of the relation of I 4.0 with the sustainable commercial model. The customer and supply chain are also digitally connected through I 4.0. For such incorporated business models that stabilize the requirement of the finance, community, and environmental issues, value proposition continues to be at the center. Both the spatial and temporal determination of these values is done.[29] Such digital and sustainable company strategies still need to be justified financially, though. (See Figure 5.3.)

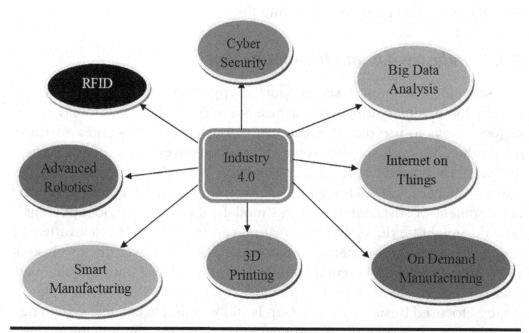

Figure 5.3 Technological pillars of industry 4.0.

5.5 Green Manufacturing Practices (GMPs) and Supply Chain Incorporated with I 4.0

Customers are seen to be at the end of a continuum that starts with suppliers. Manufacturing companies depend on distributors for basic materials and other important means from the upstream supply chain. These raw resources are transformed into final goods and given to clients. The strategic partnerships between a company and its supply chain partners have become crucial to achieving a firm's objectives in light of the expanding nature of sustainability concerns. Thus, in the context of rising environmental concerns, the role of supply chain companions (particularly, consumers and distributors) to the execution of the company cannot be overlooked. As a result, it is urgently necessary for businesses to work together along with main partners, i.e., customers and suppliers, in order to fulfill their viable objectives.[30]

For the purpose of successfully achieving their greening objectives and activities, some businesses have begun to take advantage of supply chain integration potential. For instance, large companies like Coca-Cola have undertaken initiatives that have been successful in ensuring that the corporation collaborates with business companions to manufacture eco-friendly products, reusable plastic objects extract from tress.[31]

Industry 4.0 is a concept of total point-to-point action automation along with SCM, rather than just a smart factory or smart machines. Although it is true that the process starts when a consumer needs a product, supply chain management ensures the material required to make the product is available. Supply chain management is a broad idea that is acknowledged in various ways by distinguished people. Some people only view it as the process of managing product supplies, while others see it as the interaction among the industries that provide the materials to the firms. Supply Chain 4.0 or Logistics 4.0 are the names for the smart supply chain method utilized in Industry 4.0. The emphasis of supply chain 4.0 has shifted from product delivery to pre-planning the process by examining client wants and feedback.

5.5.1 Green Supply Chain Interaction (GSCI) and Sustainable Performance

Various research has highlighted the beneficial relationship between GSCI and sustainable performance on a worldwide scale. Specifically, manufacturing companies that apply green practices like GMPs through coordination with important supply chain companion tend to improve corporate feasibility performance. In literature, various GCSI dimensions have been used to analyze the impact on feasible performance. For instance, discovering a strong correlation between GSCI variables, hence substantiating the idea that supplier integration has a substantial impact on sustainability. The financial performance of the company and EnP was found to be positively impacted by environmental transparency and green practices, such as supplier integration. GSCI is an indication that companies should utilize it in conjunction with other metrics to meet their financial and environmental objectives.[8]

5.5.2 Green Manufacturing Practices, Green Supply Chain Interaction, and Sustainable Performance

This study provides empirical evidence to support the explanatory role of the GSCI between GMPs and sustainable performance. As a result, GSCI serves as a link between GMPs and sustainable performance (indirect effect). Businesses that embrace and apply green supply chain methods, like GMPs, tend to increase their sustainable performance, according to empirical and theoretical research. The environmental cooperation that businesses have with their supply chain partners is crucial for the effective implementation of GMPs.[9] GMPs therefore have an impact on a company's sustainable performance through forging beneficial connections with supply chain associates. (See Figure 5.4.)

5.5.3 Sustainable Green Operations (GOs)

Green operations that are sustainable, GO, is a unique environmental management strategy that ensures the quality and environmental compliance of the inputs (such as metals and electronic components) and outputs (such as finished goods, carbon emissions, and trash) of electronics manufacturers. To balance and improve financial performance as well as to reduce pollution, GO places a strong emphasis on product- and process-oriented environmental practices. Product stewardship, another name for the product-oriented environmental practice of GO, aims to lessen the environmental burden by using less hazardous and non-renewable materials in the development of products. It also takes into account the environmental impact of product design, packaging, and material used. In particular, it encourages the use of green cycle parts and packaging as well as the recycling and reuse of product components with eco-design. Product stewardship of electronics producers

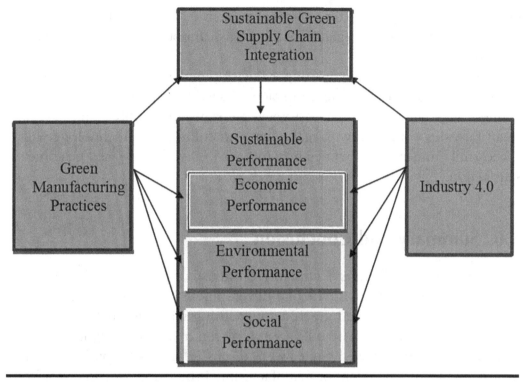

Figure 5.4   Synergistic relationships with supply chain partners.

takes into account the environmental impact of products and their packaging from the purchase of raw materials to the disposal of end-of-life products. This method aims to lessen environmental harm caused by all product-related parts and components.[32]

5.5.4 Supply Chain 4.0

Only a business with solid roots can benefit from supply chain 4.0's transformation. The correct data must be gathered in order to generate predictions; data comprising users' math scores will not be helpful in predicting their likelihood of purchasing a particular brand of toothpaste. Data doesn't communicate anything until it's transformed into information, and information is then used to generate informed business predictions. The ability to transform data into information is essential for the successful implementation of a digital company. The proper technology and software are a necessity for analytics; large data analysis is impossible without sufficient backing. Real-time data analysis is a requirement for supply chain management, and skill is needed to successfully process dynamic change and innovation. The supply chain 4.0's final pillar is its clearly defined processes for its sub-functions. The quality of the items cannot be guaranteed by an unclear process.

An organization will have stronger decision-making abilities, creative products, and end-to-end client interaction once its supply chain is clearly defined. This will ensure that customers are satisfied. Supply chain 4.0 and smart factories equipped with real talent and cutting-edge technology will successfully transition industries into Industry 4.0 with increased customer satisfaction.[32,33]

5.6 Summary and Conclusion

In order to draw the reader's attention to the use of green manufacturing, or green technology, for environmental development in the field of supply chains, this study discussed green manufacturing with sustainable supply chains and Industry 4.0. The utilization of green manufacturing, its implementation, and even its techniques were discussed in this chapter. The usage of sustainable energy, even for manufacturing, is the superior choice for both our domestic and commercial needs. The study that described the environmental management concept and its tools also addressed green operations.

The green supply chain is a highly valuable instrument since it boosts the industry's performance while enhancing the green brand and competitive edge. Future joint research projects will concentrate on finding ways to incorporate fixed costs into the decision-making process as well as incorporating a wider range of quantifiable green techniques into production, such as lighting, HVAC, or pressured air use.

The emphasis has turned more toward developing Industrial Revolution 4.0 as a result of technical advancements, inventions, and creative ideas, and this revolution is growing more complex and diverse every day. Industry 4.0 is primarily a development of cyber-physical systems, smart factories, and IoT. All of this has raised the bar for this revolution. In this chapter, we've learned how industrial revolutions have developed and how technological advances have supported, automated, and dynamically reconfigured production processes, which have hailed talent and corporate growth. With the help of technologies like artificial intelligence, cloud computing, social media analytics, big data analytics, etc., these expansions, advancements, and production are managed fairly successfully. The coordinated effort of all of these has abruptly shifted in the direction of intelligent and gradual automation. We have learned about the paradigms of Industry 4.0 in this chapter, along with some of its main goals and contemporarily relevant viewpoints. We might say that Industry 4.0 is evolving more quickly and is currently in a transitional stage, though it has not yet reached its full potential. Due to the growing technological demands of society and lessons learned from the collective intelligence features of Industry 4.0, we are aiming to enter the era of Industry 5.0, which will be more focused on customized manufacturing dependent upon the interaction and collaboration between humans and machines.

References

1. Boks, C., Nilsson, J., Masui, K., Suzuki, K., Rose, C., & Lee, B. H. (1998, May). An international comparison of product end-of-life scenarios and legislation for consumer electronics. In *Proceedings from the IEEE Symposium on Electronics and the Environment* (Vol. 19, p. 24).
2. Bowen, F. E., Cousins, P. D., Lamming, R. C., & Farukt, A. C. (2001). The role of supply management capabilities in green supply. *Production and Operations Management, 10*(2), 174–189.
3. Callahan, J. S., Dunne, R. A., & Stanaback, S. (1997). New Jersey County dismantles recycling and emissions problems. *World Wastes, 40*(3), 7–8.
4. Wong, C. W., Lai, K. H., Shang, K. C., Lu, C. S., & Leung, T. K. P. (2012). Green operations and the moderating role of environmental management capability of suppliers on manufacturing firm performance. *International Journal of Production Economics, 140*(1), 283–294.
5. Christmann, P. (2000). Effects of "best practices" of environmental management on cost advantage: The role of complementary assets. *Academy of Management Journal, 43*(4), 663–680.
6. Chung, C. J., & Wee, H. M. (2008). Green-component life-cycle value on design and reverse manufacturing in semi-closed supply chain. *International Journal of Production Economics, 113*(2), 528–545.
7. Corbett, C. J., & Klassen, R. D. (2006). Extending the horizons: Environmental excellence as key to improving operations. *Manufacturing & Service Operations Management, 8*(1), 5–22.
8. Zhu, Q., Sarkis, J., & Lai, K. H. (2007). Initiatives and outcomes of green supply chain management implementation by Chinese manufacturers. *Journal of Environmental Management, 85*(1), 179–189.
9. Kagermann, H., Helbig, J., Hellinger, A., & Wahlster, W. (2013). *Recommendations for implementing the strategic initiative INDUSTRIE 4.0: Securing the future of German manufacturing industry: Final report of the Industrie 4.0 Working Group.* Forschungsunion.

10. Dechant, K., & Altman, B. (1994). Environmental leadership: From compliance to competitive advantage. *Academy of Management Perspectives, 8*(3), 7–20.

11. Ferguson, M. E., & Toktay, L. B. (2006). The effect of competition on recovery strategies. *Production and Operations Management, 15*(3), 351–368.

12. Hunt, C. B., & Auster, E. R. (1990). Proactive environmental management: Avoiding the toxic trap. *MIT Sloan Management Review, 31*(2), 7.

13. Paul, I. D., Bhole, G. P., & Chaudhari, J. R. (2014). A review on green manufacturing: It's important, methodology and its application. *Procedia Materials Science, 6*, 1644–1649.

14. King, A. (2007). Cooperation between corporations and environmental groups: A transaction cost perspective. *Academy of Management Review, 32*(3), 889–900.

15. Kovács, G. (2008). Corporate environmental responsibility in the supply chain. *Journal of Cleaner Production, 16*(15), 1571–1578.

16. Lai, K. H., Lun, V. Y., Wong, C. W., & Cheng, T. C. E. (2011). Green shipping practices in the shipping industry: Conceptualization, adoption, and implications. *Resources, Conservation and Recycling, 55*(6), 631–638.

17. Lee, S. Y., & Klassen, R. D. (2008). Drivers and enablers that foster environmental management capabilities in small-and medium-sized suppliers in supply chains. *Production and Operations Management, 17*(6), 573–586.

18. Min, H., & Galle, W. P. (2001). Green purchasing practices of US firms. *International Journal of Operations & Production Management, 21*(9), 1222–1238.

19. Diaz-Elsayed, N., Jondral, A., Greinacher, S., Dornfeld, D., & Lanza, G. (2013). Assessment of lean and green strategies by simulation of manufacturing systems in discrete production environments. *CIRP Annals, 62*(1), 475–478.

20. Zhu, Q., & Sarkis, J. (2004). Relationships between operational practices and performance among early adopters of green supply chain management practices in Chinese manufacturing enterprises. *Journal of Operations Management, 22*(3), 265–289.

21. Pagell, M., Krumwiede, D. W., & Sheu, C. (2007). Efficacy of environmental and supplier relationship investments—moderating effects of external environment. *International Journal of Production Research, 45*(9), 2005–2028.

22. Porter, M., & Van der Linde, C. (1995). Green and competitive: Ending the stalemate. *The Dynamics of the Eco-efficient Economy: Environmental Regulation and Competitive Advantage, 33*, 120–134.

23. Preuss, L. (2001). In dirty chains? Purchasing and greener manufacturing. *Journal of Business Ethics, 34*, 345–359.

24. Rogers, D. S., & Tibben-Lembke, R. (2001). An examination of reverse logistics practices. *Journal of Business Logistics, 22*(2), 129–148.

25. Lin, R. J., Chen, R. H., & Nguyen, T. H. (2011). Green supply chain management performance in automobile manufacturing industry under uncertainty. *Procedia-Social and Behavioral Sciences, 25*, 233–245.

26. Russo, M. V., & Fouts, P. A. (1997). A resource-based perspective on corporate environmental performance and profitability. *Academy of Management Journal, 40*(3), 534–559.

27. Sarkis, J., Zhu, Q., & Lai, K. H. (2011). An organizational theoretic review of green supply chain management literature. *International Journal of Production Economics, 130*(1), 1–15.

28. Srivastava, S. K. (2007). Green supply-chain management: a state-of-the-art literature review. *International Journal of Management Reviews, 9*(1), 53–80.

29. Vachon, S., & Klassen, R. D. (2007). Supply chain management and environmental technologies: the role of integration. *International Journal of Production Research, 45*(2), 401–423.

30. Tan, X. C., Liu, F., Cao, H. J., & Zhang, H. (2002). A decision-making framework model of cutting fluid selection for green manufacturing and a case study. *Journal of Materials Processing Technology, 129*(1-3), 467–470.

31. Zhu, Q., Sarkis, J., & Lai, K. H. (2007). Green supply chain management: pressures, practices and performance within the Chinese automobile industry. *Journal of Cleaner Production, 15*(11-12), 1041–1052.

32. Tjahjono, B., Esplugues, C., Ares, E., & Pelaez, G. (2017). What does industry 4.0 mean to supply chain?. *Procedia Manufacturing, 13*, 1175–1182.

33. Schlaepfer, R. C., Koch, M., & Merkofer, P. (2015). Industry 4.0 challenges and solutions for the digital transformation and use of exponential technologies. *Deloitte, Zurique.*

Chapter 6

Green Design and Manufacturing in the Era of Industry 4.0: Toward Waste Reduction and Sustainable Environmental

Mithilesh Kumar Sahu[1], Pardeep Bishnoi[2],
S. Jeeva Chithambaram[3], and Abhijeet Singh[2]

[1]Department of Mechanical, OP Jindal University, Raigarh, Chhattisgarh
[2]Senior IP Analyst, Clarivate Analytics, Noida
[3]Department of Civil Engineering, Sarala Birla University, Ranchi, Jharkhand

6.1 Introduction

In the era of Industry 4.0, many societal practices are unsustainable, such as the increasing demand for energy, depletion of natural resources, pollution, and climate change. To address these challenges, green design is an essential component of modern manufacturing, enabling the sustainable use of natural resources. While there is no official definition of sustainability, the World Commission on Environment and Development has described it as "meeting the needs of the present without compromising the ability of future generations to meet their own needs" [1]. This definition is particularly relevant in the context of Industry 4.0, where sustainability

DOI: 10.4324/9781003439684-6

principles must be integrated into the manufacturing process to create a more sustainable future.

In view of Industry 4.0, sustainability is a critical consideration for the long-term viability of humans on the planet. With the depletion of resources and the degradation of the environment, it is essential for the present generation to develop new strategies to sustain resources and the ecosystem. The root cause of the ecological crisis is the uncontrolled extraction of natural resources for the development of the global economy.

6.2 Relation between Resource Consumption and Economic Status

Jong-Jin Kim [2] established a strong relationship between resource consumption and economic status, with increased economic growth leading to a rise in resource consumption.

Figure 6.1 represents the correlation between the per capita income of various countries and their annual energy consumption. It illustrates that developed or industrialized counties have a higher energy consumption rate than developing countries. A similar pattern can be observed in Figure 6.2, which depicts the relation between the emission of pollution per day and

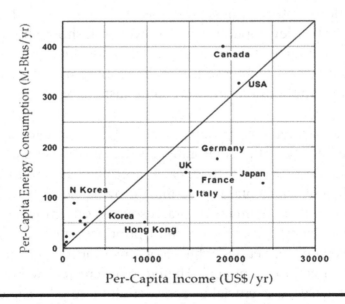

Figure 6.1   Per capita income concerning the per capita energy consumption.

Source: Courtesy of Herman Daly, Steady-State Economics *(Washington: Island Press, 1991).*

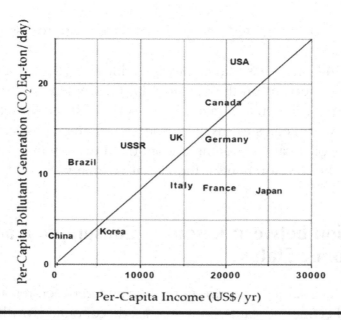

Figure 6.2   Per capita income concerning the per capita pollution generation.

Source: Courtesy of Herman Daly, Steady-State Economics (Washington: Island Press, 1991).

the per capita income. Some developed countries like Japan and China established a resource and environmental efficient structure while hovering over their economies. Both countries have very little energy consumption as well as pollution contribution as compared to the U.S.A. and Japan. The graph discusses the developed nations; however, it should be noted that the use of energy, resources like water, coal, etc., and the global share of pollution is expected to increase in the developing nations. Hence, it becomes very important to incorporate a sustainable culture into day-to-day life.

Sustainability, as defined by Marc A. Rosen [3], is the intersection of three critical aspects of nature: the environment, social factors, and economics. For sustainable practices to be effective, each facet must adhere to its specific objectives. The environmental factors must provide clean air and water, minimize soil pollution, optimize natural resource consumption, and enhance eco-balance efficiency. Social factors must prioritize safety, quality of life, health improvement, and ethics, while economics must focus on productivity, technology, and employment [4,5]. Therefore, to create a world with sustainable practices, it is crucial to consider all three pillars and work on them accordingly in the context of Industry 4.0 (Figure 6.3).

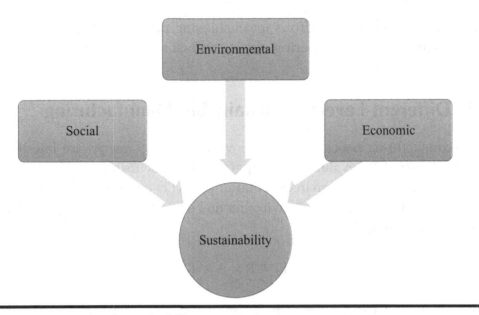

Figure 6.3   Aspects of sustainability.

6.3   Introduction to Green Design and Manufacturing

The basic aim of green design and manufacturing is to reduce the waste of materials and control the emission of greenhouse gases into the atmosphere. Materials having very high costs are thrown out into the waste, but by choosing sustainability, industries can save their energy resources and unnecessary expenses. To sustain their natural resources, the world is bending toward green design and manufacturing. Also, with eco-friendly design, industries can enhance the recycling and reuse of surplus material components. Sustainability brings innovation to manufacturing. For this movement, i.e., toward green production, technology, new methodologies, and tools are necessary to develop.

David Alan Dornfeld [6] explained various methods for enhancing resource efficiency, including: (1) Prevention of resource usage in the first place; (2) Using lighter materials; (3) Increasing resource yield; (4) Minimizing the footprint of resources; (5) Ensuring high rates of resource reuse with low associated costs; (6) Maximizing the use of existing resources; and (7) Prolonging the life span of resources.

These factors are responsible for affecting the manufacturing process, or they can be considered to originate from the modifications made in the manufacturing processes and product design. Nowadays, manufacturing companies have put their efforts into achieving profitability by increasing their productivity by considering environmental sustainability [7].

6.4 Different Levels of Sustainable Manufacturing

The manufacturing process and the environmental concerns are interlinked with each other. To evaluate the impact of manufacturing on the environment, an expression of environmental impact (EI) can be used.

A common relation for the environmental impact on society is given by the following equation [8–10]:

$$EI = P \times A \times T,$$

where P, A, and T characterize population, affluence, and technology respectively.

In the previously discussed parameter, the population and affluence of the people are increasing day by day so knowledge is the only parameter that can be manipulated to control or reduce the environmental impact [11].

Three important factors that affect the technology related to sustainable manufacturing are categories shown in Figure 6.4.

1. **Product:** The manufacturing industry makes a strategy to introduce a design process for the development of eco-friendly products. The

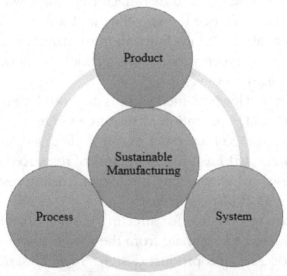

Figure 6.4 Different levels of sustainable manufacturing.

design experts use the design for environment (DFE) and to determine its impact on the environment they work on the life cycle analysis (LCA) method. By maintaining product competitiveness, flexibility in material selection also helps in the improvement of the environment.

2. **System:** Manufacturing industries use an efficient supply chain system throughout the stages of the product life cycle [12–14]. The International Organization for Standardization (ISO) develops a series of standards as an organizational guideline that focuses on their efforts on environmental management [7]. Some techniques like benchmarking and performance measurement can be used to improve the manufacturing process plan by maintaining new environmental programs and technology.

3. **Process:** By using zero-emission manufacturing, environmental issues like hazardous, toxic waste, and excess energy consumption can be controlled. It is a closed-loop manufacturing technique that maintains the industrial ecosystem by reusing wastes and by-products.

In the past, manufacturers prioritized the economic aspect of sustainability, but in recent times, they have shifted their attention to environmental sustainability. As a result, there has been a surge in the demand for tools such as life cycle assessment, design for the environment, and product management. Many instances of the application of these tools have been documented [15–17].

6.4.1 Industry 4.0: *Key Aspects and Elements of Sustainable Manufacturing*

Industry 4.0 refers to the Fourth Industrial Revolution, characterized by the integration of digital technologies into manufacturing and production processes. It encompasses various technologies such as the Internet of Things (IoT), artificial intelligence (AI), big data analytics, cloud computing, robotics, and automation. The goal of Industry 4.0 is to create smart factories and supply chains that are more efficient, flexible, and sustainable. (See Table 6.1.)

In an Industry 4.0 environment, machines and systems are interconnected and can communicate with each other and with humans in real time. This enables the collection and analysis of vast amounts of data, which can be used to optimize operations, improve decision making, and enhance productivity.

Table 6.1   Key Technologies of Industry 4.0

S. No.	Technology	Description
1	Internet of Things	Interconnectivity of devices and sensors for data exchange
2	Artificial Intelligence	Machine learning algorithms for data analysis and decision making
3	Big Data Analytics	Processing and analysis of large volumes of data
4	Robotics	Automation of tasks using robotic systems
5	Cloud Computing	Storage and processing of data in the cloud
6	Cybersecurity	Protection of data and systems from cyber threats

6.4.2 Key Aspects of Industry 4.0

a. **Connectivity:** IoT plays a crucial role in Industry 4.0, as it enables the connection of machines, sensors, and devices to gather and exchange data. This connectivity allows for real-time monitoring, control, and coordination of manufacturing processes.

b. **Data Analytics:** The availability of large amounts of data is leveraged through advanced analytics techniques, including big data analytics and AI. Data analysis provides valuable insights into process optimization, predictive maintenance, quality control, and supply chain management.

c. **Automation and Robotics:** Industry 4.0 relies heavily on automation and robotics to streamline production processes and reduce human intervention. Robotic systems can perform repetitive tasks with precision, while humans focus on more complex and creative activities.

d. **Cyber-Physical Systems (CPSs):** CPS refers to the integration of physical systems with digital technologies. It involves the use of sensors, actuators, and control systems to monitor and control physical processes. CPS enables real-time decision making and responsiveness in production environments.

e. **Smart Manufacturing:** Industry 4.0 emphasizes the concept of smart manufacturing, where intelligent systems are used to optimize the entire production life cycle. This includes product design, planning, scheduling, production, and maintenance, with a focus on resource efficiency and waste reduction.

Table 6.2   Benefits of Industry 4.0 in Sustainable Manufacturing

S. No.	Benefit	Description
1	Energy Efficiency	Optimization of energy consumption through data analysis and smart systems
2	Waste Reduction	Improved process control and predictive maintenance to minimize material waste
3	Resource Optimization	Real-time monitoring and optimization of resource usage
4	Eco-friendly Production	Implementation of sustainable practices and technologies
5	Supply Chain Visibility	Enhanced visibility of the supply chain for efficient logistics and planning
6	Product Life cycle Management	Integration of sustainability considerations throughout the product life cycle

f. **Supply Chain Integration:** Industry 4.0 promotes the integration and transparency of supply chains through digital technologies. This allows for real-time tracking of inventory, demand forecasting, efficient logistics, and improved collaboration between suppliers, manufacturers, and customers.

g. **Sustainability and Environmental Impact:** Industry 4.0 technologies can contribute to sustainability goals by enabling better resource utilization, energy efficiency, waste reduction, and environmental monitoring. The ability to gather and analyze data in real time facilitates the identification of areas for improvement and the implementation of eco-friendly practices.

These are just some of the key aspects of Industry 4.0. By leveraging advanced digital technologies and embracing the principles of sustainability, green design, and waste reduction, Industry 4.0 aims to transform traditional manufacturing into a more sustainable and environmentally friendly process. (See Table 6.2.)

6.4.3 Key Elements of Sustainable Manufacturing in Industry 4.0

a. **Energy efficiency:** The use of smart technologies and processes to optimize energy usage and reduce waste.

b. **Material efficiency:** Minimizing the use of raw materials by optimizing processes, recycling and reusing materials, and reducing waste.

c. **Green design:** The design of products and processes that minimize environmental impact, such as using eco-friendly materials and reducing emissions.

d. **Circular economy:** Adopting a closed-loop system where products are designed for reuse, repair, and recycling, to minimize waste and maximize resource efficiency.

e. **Smart supply chains:** The integration of technologies such as Internet of Things (IoT), big data analytics, and blockchain to optimize supply chain efficiency and reduce waste.

f. **Social responsibility:** Ensuring that manufacturing practices are ethical and socially responsible, including fair labor practices, human rights, and community engagement.

Figure 6.5. shows the trend of stakeholders' interest in different manufacturing techniques. Sustainable manufacturing is the latest and the most developed way to produce products, developed after a series of improvements in traditional manufacturing techniques [18,19].

Several models are utilized to enhance sustainability in manufacturing. One such model is the environmental health and safety technology engagement model proposed by Harland et al. [20], which illustrates how sustainability

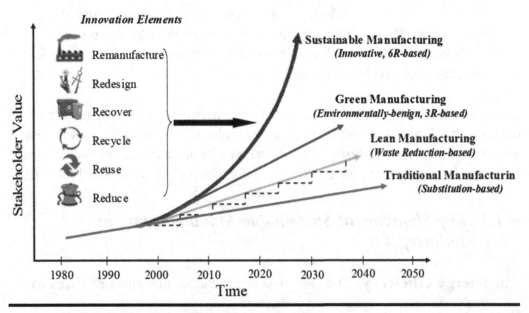

Figure 6.5   Different generation of manufacturing.

Source: Courtesy of Jawahir and Dillon (2007).

objectives can be integrated into product and process development. The study also highlights the need for a long-term commitment to environmental considerations throughout the entire design process, instead of only considering them at a single point in the product development cycle, to effectively integrate sustainability into the manufacturing process. The model is comprised of three phases, each of which provides an opportunity to address sustainability:

1. **Research:** During the research phase, the design process can be considered as per the specific sustainability requirement. These requirements may be the consumption of energy or resources, pollution, and other climatic impacts. It is the pre-competitive level stage, so environmental issues caused by manufacturing can be easily solved by doing proper research.
2. **Development:** In this stage, the major focus is on the recovery of environmental performance. Therefore, in the system design and equipment selection stages, various technologies are used, such as environmental design, life cycle assessment, etc. This phase has a very high potential for modification, which can improve sustainability.
3. **Commercialization:** Here, the efforts initiated in the development phase are improved and extended along with the involvement of suppliers, vendors, and customers.

To enhance a sustainable manufacturing system, several needs are required. These are given as:

1. **Methodology:** For this, a wide range of approaches and concepts are needed for sustainability which includes economic, social, and environmental domains along with some other relevant parameters.
2. **Methods and Tools:** For the promotion and support of sustainability, manufacturing industries have to develop and enhance smart tools and methods.
3. **Data:** To investigate the impact of sustainability on the environment and also to analyze the overall product life cycle, comprehensive and robust data is needed.
4. **Manufacturing Practices:** Practices like company policies, efforts on sustainability supportive culture, control on the environmental impact and enhance the awareness of sustainability among the customers and suppliers.

5. **Government Policies:** For the effective output of sustainability, stronger participation of government and industries is required so that they can work on incorporating the policies and programs. Cooperation between the internal and external is also needed.
6. **Research:** To explore sustainability manufacturing and design, collaborative research between industry and academia is strongly needed.

6.5 Design and Sustainability

Sustainability is an integral part of the design phase; it can be incorporated into all design phases. Several tools have been developed that can easily support these efforts. Some important design tools are discussed in this section, including design for the environment, sustainability design, and design for resources and energy.

6.5.1 Design for Environment

The main aim of the design of environment (DFE) is to reduce/control the waste of material and the emission of greenhouse gases. The cost of these waste materials is quite high; they can be reusable with certain modifications in design and manufacturing techniques. In the current era, designers have a lot of pressure of creating innovative products as well as designs that should be easy to disassemble or reuse and recycle. To determine the environmental impact of manufactured products, life cycle assessment (LCA) methods are applied to the product life cycle [21,22]. Rosen, M.A. [23] explains the four levels of LCA comprise: defining the aim and its scope, life cycle inventory analysis, assessment of its impact, and interpretation. LCA is one of the best quantitative analysis tools which studies the environmental aspects of a product throughout its life cycle, i.e., from the extraction of raw material to the decomposition or recycling of the end products. Pollution in the form of greenhouse gas emissions, solid wastes, or consumption of non-renewable resources increases the load on the environment. With the growing demand for the preservation of the environment, conservation of resources, and a sustainable society, the International Organization for Standardization (ISO) incorporated LCA into the ISO 14040 series of standards [24].

6.5.2 Design for Sustainability

Sustainability is the need to manage the available resources so that these can be shared with forthcoming generations. The term "sustainable design," also named "green design and manufacturing," assures the reduction of the excessive use of materials, energy consumption, and emission of GHG pollutants. It entails the objectives of sustainability in the design phase. Design for sustainability deals with the effect of the environment along with the optimum utilization of resources, energy, and material selection [25,26]. Also, through this design practice, industries are improving their manufacturing methods, product packaging techniques, transportation, and inventory storage [27]. It also deals with some aspects like after-sales serviceability, upgradability, and the reliability of the product [28]. The smart and advanced ways for remanufacturing and recycling are major strategic plans that come under this design technique which can boost the efficiency of manufacturing [29–31]. Hundol M.S. [32] mentioned that the designer has several tools (software like CAD/CAM and DFMA) by which they can show their creativity in green "efficient" product designs for the future generation. This research work also suggested that if possible then the designers should attempt to incorporate a concurrent engineering philosophy to aid the overall DFE effort.

In the current scenario, the interest in design for sustainability is increasing day by day. Different approaches have been reported as given here:

- Karlsson and Luuuropp [33] described an Eco-Design in which the key contributors were design, economics, and ecology.
- Borea and Wang [34] studied the correlation between quality function deployment, life cycle analysis, and contingent valuation.
- S B A Fatima et al. [35] investigate a product development approach with the integration of DFMA (Design for Manufacturing and Assembly) analysis. This approach minimizes the part number, manufacturing cost, and wastage of material.
- Although Falah Abu et al. [36] examined mathematical models using data collected from 131 lumber and furniture companies using structural equation modeling and explained the factors that constrain the implementation of lean manufacturing in the wood and furniture industries.

6.5.3 *Design for Resource and Energy*

Smith and Rees [37] studied the pattern of resource utilization as to human needs while conserving the environment so that future generations can also use these resources. The prime focus of this design process is to optimize the manpower, material, energy consumption, and other important parameters utilized in an organization and perform their task effectively with minimum wastage of natural resources. Though the sustainability of energy is a complex work, it involves the use of energy in an optimized way so that people can benefit from the energy source now and in the future. It aims at providing sufficient energy in the future for affordable necessities, is accepted by people and the community, and does not harm the environment. Letchumanan et al. [38] and Yang et al. [39] have demonstrated the implementation of green and smart manufacturing in the era of Industry 4.0.

6.6 Summary, Conclusion, and Future Directions

6.6.1 Summary

This chapter explores the intersection of green design, sustainable manufacturing, and Industry 4.0, which represents the Fourth Industrial Revolution characterized by the integration of digital technologies into manufacturing processes. The goal is to create smart factories and supply chains that are efficient, flexible, and environmentally sustainable. This chapter begins by introducing the concept of Industry 4.0 and its key technologies, including the Internet of Things (IoT), artificial intelligence (AI), big data analytics, robotics, and automation. These technologies enable real-time connectivity, data exchange, and advanced analytics for optimizing manufacturing operations.

The importance of sustainability in the manufacturing sector is highlighted, emphasizing the need for waste reduction and eco-friendly practices. Industry 4.0 offers opportunities to achieve these goals by leveraging digital technologies. It enables energy efficiency through smart energy management and optimization of resource utilization through real-time monitoring and control. This chapter discusses the benefits of Industry 4.0 in sustainable manufacturing. These include energy efficiency, waste reduction, resource optimization, eco-friendly production, supply chain visibility, and integration of sustainability throughout the product life cycle.

Furthermore, this chapter explores specific sustainable manufacturing initiatives in the context of Industry 4.0. These initiatives encompass smart energy management, predictive maintenance, circular economy practices, green supply chain integration, and life cycle assessment. Each initiative is explained in detail, highlighting its role in reducing environmental impact and promoting sustainable practices. This chapter concludes by emphasizing the transformative potential of Industry 4.0 in enabling a paradigm shift toward greener design and manufacturing. It highlights the importance of collaboration between industry stakeholders, policymakers, and researchers to drive the adoption of sustainable practices in the era of Industry 4.0.

6.6.2 Conclusion

In relation to Industry 4.0, sustainability has become a major focus area for various manufacturing processes and design techniques. The integration of sustainability principles is explored at all three levels of sustainability manufacturing: process, product, and system. Green manufacturing is a significant approach for reducing the emission of greenhouse gases, environmental pollution, and minimizing material wastage. By adopting green manufacturing practices, industries can enhance the quality and life span of their products while simultaneously reducing their environmental footprint.

Achieving sustainability in manufacturing requires several needs to be addressed, including methodology, data, research, and government policies. Sustainability must also be an integral part of the design phase, which includes design for the environment, design for sustainability, and design for resources and energy. As we move toward a sustainable future, it is important for the scientific community of both developed and developing nations to take on the challenge of green design and manufacturing, and to further boost their research in this field. With the emergence of Industry 4.0, technology can play a vital role in supporting sustainable manufacturing, through the use of smart manufacturing, predictive maintenance, and real-time data analysis.

6.6.3 Future Directions

The future directions for the present work are as follows:

a. **Emerging Technologies:** As technology continues to advance, and new innovations and technologies will emerge that can further enhance sustainability in manufacturing. Exploring and discussing these emerging technologies, such as advanced materials, nanotechnology, and biotechnology, can provide insights into their potential for waste reduction and sustainable practices.

b. **Standards and Regulations:** Governments and organizations worldwide are increasingly focusing on sustainability and enacting regulations and standards to promote environmentally responsible practices. Investigating the evolving landscape of sustainability standards and regulations relevant to Industry 4.0 can be an important aspect of future research.

c. **Life cycle Thinking:** Going beyond the traditional boundaries of manufacturing and adopting a life cycle thinking approach can help optimize the entire product life cycle from design to disposal. Future directions can involve a deeper exploration of incorporating environmental considerations throughout the life cycle, including sustainable design, product reuse, remanufacturing, and recycling.

d. **Human-Centric Approach:** While Industry 4.0 emphasizes automation and machine-centric processes, future research can explore the role of human operators in sustainable manufacturing. Understanding how human skills and expertise can be leveraged alongside digital technologies to promote sustainable practices can be an important area of investigation.

e. **Collaborative Networks:** Industry 4.0 encourages collaboration and connectivity among different stakeholders in the manufacturing ecosystem. Future directions can focus on exploring collaborative networks and partnerships between manufacturers, suppliers, customers, and research institutions to share best practices, knowledge, and resources for achieving sustainable manufacturing goals.

f. **Socio-Economic Impact:** Investigating the socio-economic impact of Industry 4.0 and sustainable manufacturing can provide valuable insights into its benefits and challenges. Future research can delve into topics such as job creation, skills development, social equity, and the economic viability of sustainable manufacturing practices.

g. **Case Studies and Success Stories:** In order to inspire and motivate stakeholders, future directions can involve showcasing real-world case studies and success stories of organizations that have successfully implemented Industry 4.0 principles for waste reduction and sustainable manufacturing. These examples can serve as practical guides and sources of inspiration for others.

By focusing on these future directions, this work can contribute to ongoing research and provide valuable insights into the evolving landscape of green design and sustainable manufacturing in the era of Industry 4.0.

References

1. Jawahir, I. S. (2008, August). Beyond the 3R's: 6 R concepts for next generation manufacturing: Recent trends and case studies. In Symposium on sustainability and product development, IIT: Chicago.

2. Jong-Jin, K., Sustainable Architecture Module: Introduction to Sustainable Design.
3. Rosen, M. A., & Kishawy, H. A. (2012). Sustainable manufacturing and design: Concepts, practices and needs. Sustainability, 4(2), 154–174.
4. Epstein, M. J., & Buhovac, A. R. (2014). Making sustainability work: Best practices in managing and measuring corporate social, environmental, and economic impacts. Berrett-Koehler Publishers.
5. Jawahir, I. S., & Dillon Jr, O. W. (2007, October). Sustainable manufacturing processes: New challenges for developing predictive models and optimization techniques. In Proceedings of the first international conference on sustainable manufacturing, Montreal, Canada (pp. 1–19).
6. Dornfeld, D. A, Moving toward Green and Sustainable Manufacturing.
7. Sarkis, J. (2001). Manufacturing's role in corporate environmental sustainability: Concerns for the new millennium. International Journal of Operations & Production Management.
8. Graedel, T. E., Allenby, B. R. (2010). Industrial ecology and sustainable engineering, Prentice Hall: Upper Saddle River, NJ, USA.
9. Hart, S. L. (1997). Beyond greening: strategies for a sustainable world. Harvard Business Review, 75(1), 66–77.
10. Johnson, D. D., & Srivastava, R. (2008, November). Design for sustainability: Product development tools and life cycle economics. In Proceedings of the 39th Annual Meeting of the Decision Sciences Institute (pp. 1711–1716).
11. MacAvoy, T. C. (1990). Technology strategies case notes, Darden School of Management, University of Virginia: Charlottesville, VA, USA.
12. Rosen, M. A., Nazzal, Y. (2013). Energy sustainability: A key to addressing environmental, economic and societal challenges. Res. J. Environ. Earth Sci., 5, 181–188.
13. Garetti, M., & Taisch, M. (2012). Sustainable manufacturing: Trends and research challenges. Production Planning & Control, 23(2-3), 83–104.
14. Badurdeen, F., Iyengar, D., Goldsby, T. J., Metta, H., Gupta, S., & Jawahir, I. S. (2009). Extending total life-cycle thinking to sustainable supply chain design. International Journal of Product Lifecycle Management, 4(1-3), 49–67.
15. Tien, S. W., Chung, Y. C., & Tsai, C. H. (2002). Environmental design implementation in Taiwan's industries. Environmental Impact Assessment Review, 22(6), 685–702.
16. Schenck, R. (2000). Using LCA for procurement decisions: A case study performed for the US Environmental Protection Agency. Environmental Progress, 19(2), 110–116.
17. Yano, M., & Kamiya, K. (2000). The national LCA project in Japan. Environmental Progress, 19(2), 140–145.
18. Krajnik, P., Pusavec, F., & Rashid, A. (2011). Nanofluids: Properties, applications and sustainability aspects in materials processing technologies. In Advances in Sustainable Manufacturing (pp. 107–113). Springer: Berlin, Heidelberg.

19. Hartini, S., & Ciptomulyono, U. (2015). The relationship between lean and sustainable manufacturing on performance: Literature review. Procedia Manufacturing, 4, 38–45.
20. Harland, J., Reichelt, T., & Yao, M. (19–22 May 2008). Environmental sustainability in the semiconductor industry. In Proceedings of the IEEE Symposium on Electronics and the Environment, San Francisco, CA, USA, (pp. 1–6).
21. Kreiger, M. A., Mulder, M. L., Glover, A. G., & Pearce, J. M. (2014). Life cycle analysis of distributed recycling of post-consumer high density polyethylene for 3-D printing filament. Journal of Cleaner Production, 70, 90–96.
22. Moro Piekarski, C., Mendes da Luz, L., Zocche, L., & De Francisco, A. C. (2013). Life cycle assessment as entrepreneurial tool for business management and green innovations. Journal of Technology Management & Innovation, 8(1), 44–53.
23. Rosen, M. A. (2002). Energy efficiency and sustainable development. International Journal of Global Energy Issues, 17(1-2), 23–34.
24. International Organization for Standardization. (2006). Environmental Management: Life Cycle Assessment; Principles and Framework (Vol. 14044). ISO.
25. Bhamra, T., & Lofthouse, V. (2016). Design for sustainability: A practical approach, Routledge: Abingdon, UK.
26. El-Halwagi, M. M. (2017). Sustainable design through process integration: Fundamentals and applications to industrial pollution prevention, resource conservation, and profitability enhancement. Butterworth-Heinemann.
27. Anderson, D. M. (2020). Design for manufacturability: How to use concurrent engineering to rapidly develop low-cost, high-quality products for lean production. CRC press.
28. Arnette, A. N., Brewer, B. L., & Choal, T. (2014). Design for sustainability (DFS): The intersection of supply chain and environment. Journal of Cleaner Production, 83, 374–390.
29. Veelaert, L., Du Bois, E., Hubo, S., Van Kets, K., & Ragaert, K. (2017). Design from recycling. In International Conference 2017 of the Design Research Society Special Interest Group on Experiential Knowledge (EKSIG).
30. Taghipour, A., Abed, M., & Zoghlami, N. (2015, May). Design for remanufacturing respecting reverse logistics processes: A review. In 2015 4th International Conference on Advanced Logistics and Transport (ICALT) (pp. 299–304). IEEE.
31. Prendeville, S., & Bocken, N. (2017). Design for remanufacturing and circular business models. In Sustainability through innovation in product life cycle design (pp. 269–283). Springer: Singapore.
32. Hundal, M. (Ed.). (2001). Mechanical life cycle handbook: Good environmental design and manufacturing. CRC Press.
33. Karlsson, R., & Luttropp, C. (2006). EcoDesign: What's happening? An overview of the subject area of EcoDesign and of the papers in this special issue. Journal of Cleaner Production, 14(15-16), 1291–1298.
34. Bovea, M. D., & Wang, B. (2007). Redesign methodology for developing environmentally conscious products. International Journal of Production Research, 45(18-19), 4057–4072.

35. Fatima, S. B. A., Effendi, M. S. M., & Rosli, M. F. (2018, November). Design for manufacturing and assembly: A review on integration with design sustainability. In AIP Conference Proceedings (Vol. 2030, No. 1, p. 020070). AIP Publishing LLC.
36. Abu, F., Gholami, H., Saman, M. Z. M., Zakuan, N., Streimikiene, D., & Kyriakopoulos, G. L. (2021). An SEM approach for the barrier analysis in lean implementation in manufacturing industries. Sustainability, 13(4).
37. Smith, C., & Rees, G. (1998). Economic Development, 2nd ed., Macmillan: Basingstoke, UK.
38. Letchumanan, L. T., Gholami, H., Yusof, N. M., Ngadiman, N. H. A. B., Salameh, A. A., Štreimikienė, D., & Cavallaro, F. (2022). Analyzing the factors enabling green lean six sigma implementation in the industry 4.0 Era. Sustainability, 14(6), 3450.
39. Yang, L., Zou, H., Shang, C., Ye, X., & Rani, P. (2023). Adoption of information and digital technologies for sustainable smart manufacturing systems for industry 4.0 in small, medium, and micro enterprises (SMMEs). Technological Forecasting and Social Change, 188, 122308.

Chapter 7

Industry 4.0 in Waste Management for Sustainable Development

Pratibha Sukla Tripathi, Govind Sahu, and Ajay Tripathi

7.1 Sustainable Development

The idea behind sustainable development is meeting current needs without sacrificing the ability of future generations to meet their own needs.[1] It is a comprehensive and integrated strategy that aims to strike a balance between economic, social, and environmental factors in order to improve everyone's quality of life while protecting the planet's ecosystems and natural resources. The "three pillars" of sustainability, including economic, social, and environmental, are frequently used to describe sustainable development, which has many different aspects.[2]

7.1.1 Principles and Components of Sustainable Development[3–5]

- **Economic Sustainability:** For raising living standards and eliminating poverty, economic development and growth are essential. However, the concept of sustainable development implies the economy must be implemented in a manner that fosters prosperity over time, decreases discrepancies, and reduces adverse environmental effects.

DOI: 10.4324/9781003439684-7

- **Social Equity:** Sustainable development must prioritize social justice and equity. This involves dealing with problems like poverty, inequality, access to healthcare, education, and fundamental human rights. Sustainable development attempts to establish equitable communities where everyone has the chance to succeed.
- **Environmental Protection:** The fundamental component of sustainable development is environmental sustainability. It entails reducing waste and depletion of resources, restoring and safeguarding ecosystems, and preserving biodiversity. To combat climate change and save the environment, it is crucial to implement policies that decrease waste, support renewable energy sources, and place restrictions on greenhouse gas emissions.
- **Interdependence:** The interrelationship among issues pertaining to the economy, society, and the environment is acknowledged in sustainable development. A comprehensive strategy is required to reconcile conflicting priorities because decisions taken in one area might have repercussions in other areas and across all dimensions.
- **Long-Term Perspective:** Making decisions with the long-term view is supported by sustainable development. This entails adopting measures to make sure facilities are utilized safely and effectively as well as taking into account how current activities may have an influence on generations to come.
- **Participation and Collaboration:** In order to achieve sustainable development, decision-making processes must involve all relevant parties, including local communities, corporations, governments, and civil society. The teamwork and cooperation are crucial for complicated issues that must be fully solved.
- **Innovation and Technology:** In order to achieve the goals of sustainable development, innovation is essential. Solutions to immediate issues, like green energy, efficient utilization of resources, and agricultural sustainability can be found in advances in technology.
- **Global Cooperation:** Global issues like biodiversity loss and climate change are just two examples of sustainability challenges. To successfully address these issues and encourage shared responsibility, international collaboration and agreements are essential.
- **Cultural Respect:** To achieve sustainable development, it is crucial to acknowledge and respect cultural diversity. Cultural norms, customs, and indigenous knowledge can help create more lasting and acceptable solutions for the situation.

7.2 Industry 4.0

The Fourth Industrial Revolution, or Industry 4.0, is the combination of digital technology, data analysis, and powerful automation in a variety of industries. It marks a substantial change in how businesses run, make things, and provide services. By utilizing technologies such as the Internet of Things (IoT), artificial intelligence (AI), machine learning, robotics, and big data to develop more effective, connected, and smart manufacturing processes, Industry 4.0 builds on the accomplishments of earlier industrial revolutions.[6]

7.2.1 Characteristics and Components of Industry 4.0[7]

- **Interconnectivity:** The IoT is used to connect systems, machines, and devices, which is a key component of Industry 4.0. This permits real-time information exchange and interaction, improving collaboration and decision making.
- **Data Analytics:** Data is a key resource for Industry 4.0. Huge amounts of data from sensors and devices are processed by advanced artificial intelligence (AI) and analytics algorithms to gain insights, improve workflows, and forecast outcomes.[7]
- **Advanced Automation:** Industry 4.0 places a lot of emphasis on automation technology, such as robotics and autonomous systems. These innovations boost productivity, cut down on mistakes, and take care of monotonous duties, leaving human beings for more difficult and imaginative jobs.
- **Digital Twin:** A virtual clone of a real-world system, procedure, or product is known as a digital twin. It enables businesses to optimize operations, fix problems, and enhance designs before deployment by enabling continuous surveillance, analysis, and simulation.
- **Smart Factories:** The development of automated factories with networked machinery is a key component of Industry 4.0. This makes production processes more flexible, customizable, and responsive.
- **Decentralized Decision Making:** Decision making may be decentralized using real-time information and analytics, enabling frontline staff to make wise decisions based on precise insights.
- **Cybersecurity:** Cybersecurity is a major concern as industries grow more digitally connected. For Industry 4.0 technologies to operate as intended, it is crucial to safeguard critical data and systems from online threats.

- **Supply Chain Optimization:** Better supply chain visibility and management are made possible by Industry 4.0 technologies. As a result, lead times are shortened and overall efficiency is increased, improving inventory management.
- **Customization and Personalization:** Greater personalization and customization of goods and services are made possible by Industry 4.0. Companies can adjust their services to specific customer preferences using insights based on data.
- **Sustainability:** By maximizing resource utilization, decreasing waste, and limiting environmental impacts through effective production processes, Industry 4.0 may support sustainability goals.
- **Skills and Workforce:** An Industry 4.0 environment requires personnel with a combination of technological and digital abilities. To use and manage innovative technologies, employees must learn new skills and adapt to shifting roles.

7.3 Waste Management

The term "waste management" refers to the accumulating, transport processing, disposing of waste.[8] In order to protect our environment, public health, and resources of nature, effective waste management is crucial. Waste management aims to reduce waste's adverse environmental impacts and encourage sustainable behaviors[9,10] (Figure 7.1).

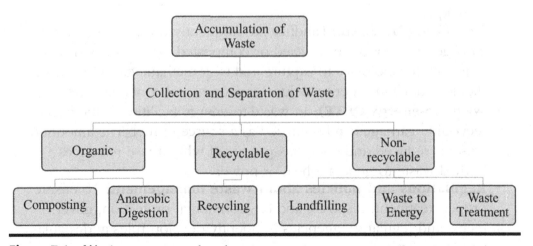

Figure 7.1 Waste management system.

- **Accumulation of waste:** Waste materials are first formed during this stage. Waste may be produced by institutional, commercial, industrial, and domestic sources.
- **Collection of waste:** Collection entails gathering waste via different sources and delivering it to specific facilities for additional processing.
- **Sorting and separation of waste:** The collected waste is sorted and divided into various categories, such as recyclables, non-recyclable waste, and organic waste, in many waste management systems. This separation increases resource recovery while decreasing the amount of waste sent to landfills or burned.
- **Recycling of waste:** To save resources and energy, recyclable materials can be processed and used again, such as paper, cardboard, glass, plastics, and metals. Recycling lessens the need for fresh production and has a smaller negative impact on the environment.
- **Composting of waste:** Composting can be used to make soil amendments that are rich in nutrients from organic waste, including food leftovers and yard clippings. Composting increases soil health and decreases landfill waste.

$$\text{Organic matter} + O_2 \rightarrow \text{Compost} + CO_2 + H_2O + NO_3 + SO_4 + \text{Heat}$$

- **Treatment of waste:** Prior to disposal, some wastes, such as hazardous waste and medical waste, need to undergo particular processing to eliminate any dangerous qualities. Burning, chemical reactions, and biological processes are all examples of treatment techniques.
- **Landfilling by waste:** Landfills are frequently used to dispose of garbage that cannot be recycled or composted. Modern landfills are built with technologies to capture and treat methane gas and leachate (liquid runoff) in order to reduce environmental contamination.
- **Waste-to-energy (WTE):** In waste-to-energy facilities, some non-recyclable garbage can be utilized as a source of fuel. The amount of waste is reduced and energy is produced when these resources burned waste to generate heat or power.
- **Regulations and policies about waste management:** To ensure proper treatment, disposal, and environmental protection, governments and regulatory agencies frequently develop rules and regulations for waste management.

- **Public education and awareness:** Effective waste management involves increasing attention and nurturing people regarding minimizing waste, recycling, and responsible disposal techniques.

7.3.1 Waste Management and Industry 4.0

Waste management is one of the areas that can benefit significantly from the integration of Industry 4.0 technologies. Automation, data analytics, and advanced digital technologies can improve the efficacy, sustainability, and efficiency of waste management systems. Here is how waste management can benefit from Industry 4.0:[11]

- **Smart Waste Collection:** Waste bins and containers can use sensors and Internet of Things (IoT) devices to track fill levels in real time. By using this information, waste collection routes can be improved, saving fuel and lowering vehicle emissions. Additionally, smart collection stops overflows and guarantees prompt pickups.
- **Predictive Maintenance:** For waste collection equipment and vehicles, Industry 4.0 technologies provide predictive maintenance. In order to prevent breakdowns and downtime, sensors can monitor the health of machinery and vehicles.
- **Data-Driven Decision Making:** Decision-makers can learn more about waste creation trends, recycling rates, disposal costs, and other topics by gathering and evaluating data from different waste management processes. Decision making is made more informed and efficient thanks to this data-driven methodology.
- **Resource Optimization:** Waste management organizations may improve the allocation of resources by using AI and data analytics. This involves anticipating when containers need to be emptied, choosing the most effective disposal techniques, and better managing recyclables.
- **Waste Sorting and Recycling:** Industry 4.0–enabled automated sorting technology can improve recycling facilities. Different sorts of materials can be sorted effectively by robots and AI-powered systems, increasing recycling rates and lowering pollution.
- **Waste-to-Energy Conversion:** By maximizing the process of combustion and energy output, Industry 4.0 technology can improve waste-to-energy facilities. While reducing their negative effects on

the environment, continuous time control and monitoring equipment can guarantee optimal energy output.

- **Sustainability Reporting:** Tools from Industry 4.0 allow for precise and automatic data collection for reports on sustainability. Trash management businesses can monitor and report on important indicators such as fees, reduction of greenhouse gas emissions, and energy recovery.

- **Traceability and Accountability:** The transportation of waste can be monitored transparently and auditable using blockchain technology. Decreasing the risk of unlawful dumping and encouraging appropriate disposal, improves credibility in the method used for management of waste.

- **Public Engagement:** To involve the public in waste reduction and recycling activities, internet-based platforms, apps, and communication devices can be used. Industry 4.0 can promote consciousness-raising and environmentally friendly behavior by offering real-time data and instructional opportunities.

- **Circular Economy Initiatives:** By facilitating improved material monitoring and life cycle management, Industry 4.0 promotes the circular economy. This facilitates industry and consumer decision making that encourages recycling and reuse.

Waste management that adheres to Industry 4.0 principles increases operational effectiveness while also promoting resource efficiency and environmental sustainability. Waste management may become more adaptable, data-driven, and sensitive to the problems of a quickly changing environment by embracing digital technologies.

7.3.2 Application of Industry 4.0 in Waste Management for Sustainable Development

Industry 4.0, sustainable development, and waste management are all interconnected and can be used in concert to build systems that are more effective, environmentally friendly, and socially responsible. The connections between these three ideas are as follows:[11]

- **Efficiency and Resource Optimization:** The effectiveness of waste management procedures is improved by Industry 4.0 technologies. Real-time monitoring, data analytics, and intelligent waste collection improve waste collection routes, save fuel use, and lower operational expenses. This effectiveness supports economic sustainability, a crucial component of sustainable development.

- **Environmental Impact Reduction:** Systems for waste management can reduce their environmental impact with the help of Industry 4.0. The carbon footprint and pollutants linked to waste management can be decreased by maximizing waste collection, treatment, and disposal. The environmental component of sustainable development is supported by this.
- **Circular Economy Promotion:** By enhancing material sorting, recycling, and reuse, Industry 4.0 aids in the shift to a circular economy. This lessens the demand for raw resources and lessens the industrial process's overall impact on the environment. The objective of responsible production and consumption under sustainable development is aligned with a circular economy strategy.
- **Innovation and Technological Advancement:** Industry 4.0 promotes waste management innovation, which results in the creation of novel methods and technologies. These inventions promote ongoing progress in resource saving, waste reduction, and environmental protection. These all are the essential elements of sustainable development.
- **Data-Driven Decision Making:** Decisions about waste management are influenced by the data gathered and examined by Industry 4.0 technology. Insights into garbage creation trends, rates of recycling, and impact on the environment are provided by this data, enabling for better informed and successful solutions to promote sustainable growth goals.
- **Public Engagement and Awareness:** Real-time data sharing made possible by Industry 4.0 can be utilized to engage the public and spread awareness of waste minimization, reuse and recycling, and sustainable consumption. By encouraging informed and ethical behavior, public education supports the social dimension of sustainable development.
- **Social Benefits:** By automating repetitive and physically draining operations, Industry 4.0 technology can enhance the working environment for waste management workers. By improving safety for employees and job satisfaction, this improves societal well-being.
- **Long-Term Planning and Risk Mitigation:** The tools for strategic planning and risk reduction in waste management are provided by Industry 4.0 technology. Real-time monitoring and predictive analytics help foresee problems, avert waste-related emergencies, and

guarantee the sustainability of waste management procedures over the long term.

- **Partnerships and Collaboration:** Collaboration between governmental organizations, for-profit businesses, and academic institutions is frequently necessary for the integration of Industry 4.0 into waste management. Such partnerships encourage information exchange, capacity development, and teamwork in the pursuit of objective of sustainable development.

By enhancing economic effectiveness, saving the environment, and community well-being, the incorporation of Industry 4.0 concepts into the management of waste supports sustainable development. The concepts of a sustainable and just future can be more adaptable, resource-efficient, and in line with waste management methods by utilizing cutting-edge technologies.

Industry 4.0 became famous after 2011, which is also considered the Fourth Industrial Revolution. The goal of Industry 4.0 is to produce as much as possible and to maximize profits, however doing so has detrimental effects on other areas, including the environment due to the degradation of renewable resources, poor working conditions, and unequal wealth distribution. As a result, consumption patterns become unsustainable from an economic, environmental, and social standpoint.[12,13] Although the production system has some drawbacks—the environment is not sustainable, trash is not recycled, and products are not based on the renewable concept—we must not disregard the fact that our system is capable of handling such waste. Because production belongs to a model with "weak sustainability," it mismanages the balance of natural resources or waste management by producing items that are environmentally disposable.[14] As a result, we should place an emphasis on renewable resources rather than nonrenewable ones. There is a significant difference among real and sustainable usage because the actual requirement for the items and things is substantially lower than the demand.[15] This condition will cause a decrease in natural resources, damaging the ecology and biodiversity.[16] The past research has shown that environmental concerns are very important, but at the same time, innovative technologies such as Industry 4.0 will result in products of greater quality.[17] Environmental sustainability is less of an issue in Industry 4.0 because its main goals are to enhance output, improve quality, and raise income. The lack of competent labor, organizational norms, and a sustainable framework are some of the difficulties the Industrial Revolution is currently confronting.[18] The methods and processes of production have completely been altered as a result

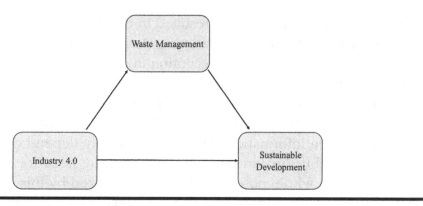

Figure 7.2   Theoritical framework.

of Industry 4.0.[19] Industry 4.0 technology has a cheap cost of manufacturing, but it is difficult to gauge its immediate influence on environmental sustainability.[20] We therefore need to understand how Industry 4.0 will affect environmental sustainability and society.

Here, the 3Rs—reduce, reuse, and recycle—of waste management environmental education become necessary. Utilizing things more than once and recycling them will aid in reducing overproduction. The optimum use of resources and ultimately, sustainability may result from this. This study will examine sustainability in terms of the economy, society, and environment. The niche theory and the CPS form the foundation of the study's theoretical framework.[21] G. Evelyn Hutchinson first proposed the idea of the niche in 1957. This hypothesis talked about how the world's population is expanding and how renewable resources and species are disappearing. Additionally, it described how rivals, populations, and living things react to the loss of resources. It provided instructions on how to reduce waste and make the best use of the resources that are available. Mass production and personalized products are explained in order by CPS.[22] The manufacturing process and its effects on the environment will be the focus of this theory.[23] Because CPS is associated with Industry 4.0 and niche will be relevant to environmental sustainability and waste management, both theories will support the current study. (See Figure 7.2.)

7.4   Industry 4.0–Based Solid Waste Management for Sustainable Future

Since computers were first created, people have continued to expand this technology, which sparked the Third Industrial Revolution and a rush in technological development that resulted in the development of automated machines, technologies, and electronics. Despite their strength, these systems required data transmission and reception in order to interact and build more dynamic and sophisticated systems.

In order to drive smart automation made possible by modern technologies like AI and ML, IR 4.0 focuses on the networking of computer devices. It is a time when information systems that heavily depend on the IoT have been developed for making decisions without the need for human interaction. The whole potential of IR 4.0 is realized by this innovative idea of systems producing and exchanging information wirelessly. Today, automated farms in agriculture and the worldwide communications sector use this ground-breaking technology.[8,24] This doesn't end there, as newer technologies like virtual reality and self-driving cars are also being developed.[25]

The Internet of Things (IoT) is a relatively recent concept that consists of a network of linked objects that are outfitted with electronic sensors and parts that enable them to analyze data and communicate with one another on a framework, sending data via the internet. The infrastructure required to support the existence of the IoT (Wi-Fi, Bluetooth, microcontroller, etc.) has been developed as a result of developments in electronic engineering and communications technology. Kevin Ashton first used the term "Internet of Things" (IoT) in 1999 to refer to the interconnection of items with the internet.[26] Since then, the IoT has expanded into a number of sectors, including healthcare, transportation, and agriculture.[27] For example, mobile phones can be used as IoT device in the construction of smart transportation systems and can give real-time geographic location to predict traffic and compute an optimized route to cut down on travel time as well as energy use.[27] The upcoming IR 4.0 technology of additive manufacturing (AM) is a recent discovery. As a result, IoT applications can be useful for managing solid waste. Although IoT appears to be a promising technology, it has limitations if the security and privacy issues that come with it are not well addressed.[28] Furthermore, the Internet of Things provides an infrastructure for continuous surveillance applications. Utilizing IoT for solid waste management can be advantageous. As data is automatically gathered and wirelessly shared, governments and municipalities have simpler access to a richer data set, providing a more precise understanding of the whole supply chain for waste management. Future project planning and decision making are aided by the simplicity with which underlying problems can be identified.[27]

According to Kok et al. (2009),[29] artificial intelligence (AI) is the creation of computers that have the capacity to learn, make judgments without human intervention, and self-correct. By enhancing waste collection patterns based on the available data gathered in real time, this helpful tool can be employed in the handling of solid waste. A division of AI is ML. Scientists have previously referred to it as an IoT tool for predictive generation. It is a computer algorithm that can predict results based on a collection of data without having external human commands.[30] El Naqa and Murphy (2015) [31] explain how ML operates by training an algorithm to recognize patterns by parsing data. Both audio and visual data can be included in this group. A more precise forecasting algorithm will result from a larger training data collection, which may also improve decision making. According to a review, ML was used in agriculture to help assess crop quality and, in certain circumstances, even identify subspecies. From smartphones for improved photography and processing to recognizing faces utilizing deep learning artificial neural networks, it is embedded practically everywhere. More ML applications can be made possible by producing a lot of data through the use of IoT-enabled devices, where gathered information from product sensors is transferred to a centralized system to be analyzed and analyzed, as this technology performs better with a huge collection of data to train upon. Due to the expansion of data kinds that may be gathered and improved upon by current ones, this may open the door for new fields of study. Waste may be automatically categorized and sorted using machine learning in conjunction with image recognition. The contrast between IoT and AI is seen in Figure 7.3.

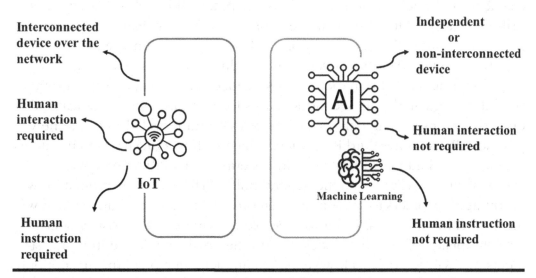

Figure 7.3   Comparison between Artificial Intelligence and Internet of Things.

The usage of additive manufacturing is one of the important and rising technologies of IR 4.0 in recent advances. The method of layer-by-layer material deposition used in additive manufacturing, sometimes referred to as 3D printing, is computerized. Complex structures that were previously too challenging to fabricate can now be produced using this innovative technique. Numerous additive manufacturing technologies that have been developed, including stereolithography (SLA), selective laser sintering (SLS), fused deposition modeling (FDM), direct metal laser sintering (DMLS), and many more.[32] Additionally, this way of producing goods will successfully reduce waste by eliminating the requirement to process the raw materials before using conventional manufacturing processes like cutting, milling, drilling, etc., and, as a result, lowering the amount of trash generated.

7.5 Summary

The Industrial Revolution significantly increased the usage of harmful chemicals and the release of pollutants, which created problems for the environment and society. Industrialization boosts a nation's economic growth and provides more revenue to the organization. However, if environmental and social concerns are neglected by a company, the industry's expansion is not helpful for such concerns. Core technologies in Industry 4.0 like IoT, AI, ML, and cloud computing were succinctly described along with their characteristics and functions as well as the potential benefits that could be realized if applied to waste management. All of the sustainable development components (the 3Rs) must be prioritized equally if sustainable development is to be achieved. The first R stands for "reduce," which means that manufacturing should only be done as needed and that excessive output should be regulated. The second R stands for recycling, which indicates that discarded items or materials should be reused and recycled to create new products. Reuse is the third R, and it emphasizes how crucial it is to use items repeatedly. Additionally, it will aid in fostering a favorable perception of the company among clients and the general public. This favorable reputation will encourage customers to place additional orders with the company, which will increase earnings. Thus, it is also possible to claim that the costs associated with the pillars of economy, society, and the environment are truly investments that will pay off in a few years. The implementation of the 3Rs not only promotes resource conservation but also offers financial rewards, which ultimately promotes sustainability. Waste management contributes to the sustainability that results in sustainable development.

References

1. Verma, A. K. (2019). Sustainable development and environmental ethics. International Journal on Environmental Sciences, 10(1), 1–5.
2. Mensah, J. (2019). Sustainable development: Meaning, history, principles, pillars, and implications for human action: Literature review. Cogent Social Sciences, 5(1), 1653531.
3. Sharma, H. B., Vanapalli, K. R., Samal, B., Cheela, V. S., Dubey, B. K., & Bhattacharya, J. (2021). Circular economy approach in solid waste management system to achieve UN-SDGs: Solutions for post-COVID recovery. Science of The Total Environment, 800, 149605.
4. Duić, N., Urbaniec, K., & Huisingh, D. (2015). Components and structures of the pillars of sustainability. Journal of Cleaner Production, 88, 1–12.
5. Jin, Z., & Bai, Y. (2011). Sustainable development and long-term strategic management: Embedding a long-term strategic management system into medium and long-term planning. World Future Review, 3(2), 49–69.
6. Sathyan, M. (2020). Chapter six-industry 4.0: Industrial internet of things (IIOT). Advances in Computers, 117, 129–164.
7. Suleiman, Z., Shaikholla, S., Dikhanbayeva, D., Shehab, E., & Turkyilmaz, A. (2022). Industry 4.0: Clustering of concepts and characteristics. Cogent Engineering, 9(1), 2034264.
8. Muangprathub, J., Boonnam, N., Kajornkasirat, S., Lekbangpong, N., Wanichsombat, A., & Nillaor, P. (2019). IoT and agriculture data analysis for smart farm. Computers and Electronics in Agriculture, 156, 467–474.
9. Demirbas, A. (2011). Waste management, waste resource facilities and waste conversion processes. Energy Conversion and Management, 52(2), 1280–1287.
10. Pujara, Y., Pathak, P., Sharma, A., & Govani, J. (2019). Review on Indian Municipal Solid Waste Management practices for reduction of environmental impacts to achieve sustainable development goals. Journal of Environmental Management, 248, 109238.
11. Javaid, M., Haleem, A., Singh, R. P., Suman, R., & Gonzalez, E. S. (2022). Understanding the adoption of Industry 4.0 technologies in improving environmental sustainability. Sustainable Operations and Computers, 3, 203–217.
12. McWilliams, A., Parhankangas, A., Coupet, J., Welch, E., & Barnum, D. T. (2016). Strategic decision making for the triple bottom line. Business Strategy and the Environment, 25(3), 193–204.
13. Bonilla, S. H., Silva, H. R., Terra da Silva, M., Franco Gonçalves, R., & Sacomano, J. B. (2018). Industry 4.0 and sustainability implications: A scenario-based analysis of the impacts and challenges. Sustainability, 10(10), 3740.

14. Zhu, D., Zhang, S., & Sutton, D. B. (2015). Linking Daly's Proposition to policymaking for sustainable development: indicators and pathways. Journal of Cleaner Production, 102, 333–341.

15. Terlau, W., & Hirsch, D. (2015). Sustainable consumption and the attitude-behaviour-gap phenomenon-causes and measurements toward sustainable development. Proceedings in Food System Dynamics, 199–214.

16. Szeremlei, A. K., & Magda, R. (2015). Sustainable production and consumption. Visegrad Journal on Bioeconomy and Sustainable Development, 4(2), 57–61.

17. Xu, L. D., Xu, E. L., & Li, L. (2018). Industry 4.0: State of the art and future trends. International Journal of Production Research, 56(8), 2941–2962.

18. Lentner, C., Vasa, L., & Zéman, Z. (2019). New dimensions of internal controls in banking after the GFC. Economic Annals-XXI, 176.

19. Shpak, N., Podolchak, N., Karkovska, V., & Sroka, W. (2019). The influence of age factors on the reform of the public service of Ukraine. Central European Journal of Public Policy, 13(2), 40–52.

20. Smith, J. A. (2011). Evaluating the contribution of interpretative phenomenological analysis: A reply to the commentaries and further development of criteria. Health Psychology Review, 5(1), 55–61.

21. Hutchinson, G. E. (1961). The paradox of the plankton. The American Naturalist, 95(882), 137–145.

22. Balasingham, K. (2016). Industry 4.0: securing the future for German manufacturing companies (Master's thesis, University of Twente).

23. Lee, E. A. (2008, May). Cyber physical systems: Design challenges. In 2008 11th IEEE International Symposium on Object and Component-oriented Real-time Distributed Computing (ISORC) (pp. 363–369). IEEE.

24. Ali, M. I., Ono, N., Kaysar, M., Shamszaman, Z. U., Pham, T. L., Gao, F., … & Mileo, A. (2017). Real-time data analytics and event detection for IoT-enabled communication systems. Journal of Web Semantics, 42, 19–37.

25. Simiscuka, A. A., Markande, T. M., & Muntean, G. M. (2019). Real-virtual world device synchronization in a cloud-enabled social virtual reality IoT network. IEEE Access, 7, 106588–106599.

26. Gokhale, P., Bhat, O., & Bhat, S. (2018). Introduction to IOT. International Advanced Research Journal in Science, Engineering and Technology, 5(1), 41–44.

27. Cheah, C. G., Chia, W. Y., Lai, S. F., Chew, K. W., Chia, S. R., & Show, P. L. (2022). Innovation designs of industry 4.0 based solid waste management: Machinery and digital circular economy. Environmental Research, 213, 113619.

28. Brous, P., Janssen, M., & Herder, P. (2020). The dual effects of the Internet of Things (IoT): A systematic review of the benefits and risks of IoT adoption by organizations. International Journal of Information Management, 51, 101952.

29. Kok, J. N., Boers, E. J., Kosters, W. A., Van der Putten, P., & Poel, M. (2009). Artificial intelligence: Definition, trends, techniques, and cases. Artificial intelligence, 1, 270–299.

30. Messaoud, S., Bradai, A., Bukhari, S. H. R., Quang, P. T. A., Ahmed, O. B., & Atri, M. (2020). A survey on machine learning in Internet of Things: Algorithms, strategies, and applications. Internet of Things, 12, 100314.
31. El Naqa, I., & Murphy, M. J. (2015). What is machine learning? (pp. 3–11). Springer International Publishing.
32. Haleem, A., & Javaid, M. (2019). Additive manufacturing applications in industry 4.0: A review. Journal of Industrial Integration and Management, 4(04), 1930001.

Chapter 8

Optimization of Thickness by Design of Experiments and Energy-Saving Techniques for Industry 4.0 in Galvanization Process: Literature Survey

Neha Verma[1], Vinay Sharma[2], and Ishwar Bhiradi[3]

[1]*Department of Mechanical Engineering, Shri Shankaracharya Institute of Professional Management and Technology, Raipur, Chhattisgarh, India*
[2]*Department of Production Engineering, Birla Institute of Technology, Mesra, Ranchi, Jharkhand, India*
[3]*Department of Mechatronics, Manipal Institute of Technology, Manipal Academy of Higher Education Manipal, Karnataka*

8.1 Introduction

The primary manufacturing sector is the steel industry, which also has a higher energy consumption than other manufacturing sectors. Steel products need to be protected from corrosion when they are placed in humid and corrosive conditions because manufacturing expenses in the steel industry are also quite costly. Steel goods are used in many different industries, including power transmission, building, production, and the automotive industry. Many steel items, such as towers for high power transmission and underground

DOI: 10.4324/9781003439684-8

pipelines, are positioned in an open environment. All these products are galvanized to protect them. In Industry 4.0, most of the galvanizing industries use the hot-dip galvanization (HDG) method of galvanization. Through dipping the surface of steel into molten zinc during the HDG manage a protective zinc coating is put on the steel surface to prevent it from corrosion. Steels are shielded from the environment by this zinc coating, which keeps the steel from corroding. The zinc coating's quality affects how resistant something is to corrosion. In the HDG, the microstructure and coating thickness are related to the coating's ability to resist corrosion [1]. The excessive coating thickness and dross buildup in the ZB kettle both enhance zinc consumption during the galvanization process [2]. The layers and flue gases of the zinc bath kettle are where energy is lost during the HDG process [3] and [4]. The overuse of assets raises production costs, which limits the ability of the industries that are galvanizing to make money. Waste products, such as low-quality coatings and needless over-coatings of zinc layers, are another cause of resource loss. The statistical method to design of experiments (DOE) is beneficial for predicting zinc layer thickness and optimizing influencing factors [5–7], as well as for resolving issues with excessive coating growth in HDG. The statistical method DOE analyzes the relevant properties and selects the best phase of characteristics to optimize. Additionally, a statistical approach offers statistical support for the conclusion, validating the findings. The DOE has used several models, including the Taguchi technique, the genetic algorithm, and the response surface methodology (RSM), among others, in the galvanization process [5]. This review chapter details the thorough analysis of various types of HDG-related literature and the corrective measures taken by researchers to enhance the HDG procedure for Industry 4.0.

8.2 Literature Review

The five key study areas for Industry 4.0 related to the HDG process are described in this review. The first three sections contain a thorough examination of the zinc bath kettle and its three key components: alloy addition, temperature, and immersion time. The optimization methods utilized in the HDG method are covered in the fourth part. Further study on the energy-saving strategy for the galvanization procedure has been covered in the fifth section.

8.2.1 Impact of HDG Bath Alloy Additions on the Coating's Thickness, Microscopic Structure, and Durability to Corrosion

Kania, Mendala, et al. [2] evaluated carefully the many aspects of alloy addition and investigated various types of literature on the impact of HDG zinc bath alloy additions on the framework and depth of the coating. They also investigated the negative impacts of alloy addition when the percentage content of the alloys is higher than the ideal level. The researchers recommend a suitable ratio of different alloys. According to them, the concentrations of lead (Pb), tin (Sn), aluminum (Al), and nickel (Ni) should be between 0.005–0.01%, 0.04–0.6%, 0.05–0.1%, 0.4–0.5%, and 0.1–0.3%, respectively. Scientists concluded that Ni only affects how reactive the Sandelin family of steels are, although Al, Sn, and Bi also contribute to maintaining the reactivity to few levels. The inclusion of Bi, Sn, and Pb additionally improves the coated surface's look. The investigators of this work offered three types of baths that are optimal: Zn-AlNiPb, Zn-AlNiBi, and Zn-AlNiBiSn [2]. Kania and Komorowski [8] also chose all three of these baths. The corrosion resistance and coating depth of samples manufactured from Sebisty steels were tested by the authors using these baths. The depth of the coating produced from the Zn-AlNiBiSn bath was the thinnest, while the thickness achieved from the pure zinc bath was the thickest. However, the corrosion resistance of the coating obtained from the Zn-AlNiand Zn-AlNiBiSn bath increased more than that of the pure zinc bath. The corrosion resistance of the Pb-containing bath decreases [8]. The Zn-AlNiPb bath has also been researched by Kania and Liberski [9], who discovered that the coating pattern produced by this bath for the Sandelin scale of steels is identical to that of low silicon steels. The claim made by the authors that this bath reduces coating thickness and, therefore, zinc utilization, is supported by the evidence. They concluded that Sandelin's effects were no longer present [9]. The identical Zn-AlNiPb bath has also been researched by Kania, Saternus, or Kudlácek [9], who contrasted the corrosion resistance of coatings made from pure zinc and Zn-AlNiPb. They utilize a sample of low silicon steel, which is steel with a silicon content of less than 0.021%. According to the authors, a pure zinc bath has greater corrosion resistance than a bath that also includes Pb, Al, and Ni. Therefore, it may be claimed that the zinc coating's ability to avert corrosion is decreased by the Pb-containing solution [9]. Kania et al. [10] worked to examine the microstructure and corrosion resistance of ZC made for low silicon steel using a Zn-AlNiBi bath. The researchers discovered that coatings made from Zn-AlNiBi exhibit lower corrosion resistance than coatings made from pure zinc bath. The researchers discovered that Bi is present at the outer surface of coating in the form of precipitates at the outer surface of the ZC by examining the microstructure of coating achieved from a bath containing Bi. The corrosion resistance of the galvanized coating is diminished because the Bi precipitates, becoming more corrosion-prone and forms corrosion cells at the outer layer [10].

Królikowska et al. [11] investigated how lead (Pb) affected coatings made during the hot-dip galvanization process. They looked at how low silicon steel and low- and high-Sebisty scale steels behaved in terms of pitting corrosion on the coated surface. The researchers looked at how a coating's life span, reliability, and quality are affected by a lead content that is too high. According to Shukla et al. [12], adding antimony (Sb) and magnesium increases corrosion resistance. The authors also recommended that bismuth (Bi) could be used in place of lead (Pb) (for endurance and environmental considerations) [11]. According to Tang [13], the inclusion of Ni in the galvanizing bath aids in lowering the reaction time of steel with less than 0.2% Si content. Additionally, they asserted that the Al addition aids in regulating reactiveness [13]. According to Saravanan and Srikanth's [14] investigation, the zinc coated surface adheres poorly to low levels of aluminum (almost 0.11%). According to O. S. Bondareva and Melnikow [15], when the percentage of nickel in the bath surpasses 0.06%, too much dross forms.

Pistofidis et al. [16] examined the impact of adding nickel and bismuth. They discovered that both alloys had several benefits, however the corrosion resistance was significantly decreased by the Bi. However, the Bi also lowers surface tension and coating thickness [16]. The combined effect of Ni and Bi alloys has also been studied by Fratesi et al. [17] through experiments in four distinct hot-dip galvanizing businesses. The reactivity of steels is regulated according to the authors' research, when Ni and Bi are utilized at 0.04% and 0.1%, respectively. Additionally, they discovered that the surface roughness of phosphorous-containing steels prevented them from being of high enough quality [17]. The impact of several zinc bath kettle alloying parts on the crystallization process and different ZC qualities was investigated by Vourlias et al. [18]. They concluded that Ni and Al alloys are what cause the external phase. While tin has no effect on the formation of the outer layer, lead (Pb) also aids in its growth. The presence of copper (Cu) alloy tempts the formation of heterogeneous nuclei [18]. Katiforis [19] has also researched the zinc coating's tendency to shatter when alloys containing tin (Sn), copper (Cu), and cadmium (Cd) are present. According to Di Cocco et al. [20],

Cu reduces the depth of the zc phase while tin (Sn) improves the reactivity, which leads to an increase in coating depth. Additionally, they asserted that Pb causes the coating architecture to become brittle, which does not occur in coating obtained from a zinc bath containing tin (Sn) [20].

8.2.2 Consequences of Silicon Content in Steels on Zinc Bath Kettle Temperature

Bondareva [21] conducts a study to examine the impact of zinc bath kettle temperature. A small number of nuts and bolts with a silicon concentration of 0.22% were employed by the author, or four temp ranges—4750°C, 4850°C, 5250°C, and 5350°C—were chosen for the investigation. According to the author, as temperature rises between 475 and 5350°C, coating thickness decreases. A higher coating excellence, like the gray color of coating with a matte and smooth surface finish, has also been accomplished at 5350°C [21]. Minimum depth has also been achieved at this temperature, and the development of phases has not been seen [22]. Olga Sergeevna Bondareva et al. [22] have also investigated how temperature affects the coating of high silicon steels and discovered that the smallest coating thickness was reached at 5550°C. According to Wang et al. [23], coating thickness grows in step with heat from 520 to 5300°C, with a minimum coating thickness at 5000°C for steel samples having 0.102% silicon. A pure iron sheet with silicon content less than 0.007% was found to have the maximum coating thickness at 4800°C by Bicao et al. [24] in their investigation. The highest coating depth for the steel sample, including 0.021% silicon, has reportedly been obtained at 5300°C, according to Verma and Van Ooij [25]. At the same temperatures, more dross forms in a high silicon alloy bath contrasted to the low silicon alloy bath, according to research by Luo et al. [26] who researched the behavior of dross production. When Tzimas and Papadimitriou [27] tested a sample of steel containing 0.027% silicon, they discovered that fracture formation starts to happen at a temperature of 560°C for a zinc bath kettle containing 99.99% pure zinc.

8.2.3 Impact of Immersion Time on the Reactivity of Steels

When immersion time is increased, coating thickness rises while hardness (Rockwell hardness) drops, according to research by Hakim et al. [28] on the impact of immersion duration on hardness, coating thickness, and microstructure in HDG. The scientists further observed that different immersion times have no impact on the microstructure [28]. In their study, Sepper et al. [29] found that for the same immersion period, silica-containing steels with a silicon content between 0.06 and 0.11% had the maximum coating thickness increase. Every steel sample did, however, increase in coating thickness for a total immersion period of 20 minutes as opposed to 3.25 minutes [29]. [2] backed with Sepper et al.'s contention or stated that steel with a Si content of 0.05% grew coatings more quickly than steel with Si contents of 0.02%, 0.18%, and 0.32%. Twelve minutes of immersion time was required to reach the maximum coating thickness. Additionally, Bondareva and Melnikov [30] found that the maximum zinc layer thickness for steel with silicon contents of 0.1% and 0.5% was attained.

8.2.4 *Design of Experiments (DOE) Optimization Approach Utilized in HDG Process*

The blocking concept of an experimental setup was employed by Fernandes et al. [7] to measure the weight of zinc on galvanized wire. ANOVA was also used by the researchers to test the null hypothesis. The full factorial experimental approach was used by Smith and Larson [31] to solve a fictitious example pertaining to the galvanization procedure as well as offer several experimental design methods. Wang [5] used three experiment design approaches to investigate what influences zinc coating thickness the greatest. These three methodologies are the Taguchi technique, the response surface technique, and the genetic algorithm, among others [5]. Shukla et al.'s [6] model of an ANN was originated to forecast the depth of the zinc layer. Taguchi's orthogonal array approach is also used by researchers to analyze sensitivity as well. The approach of studies by Michal et al. [32] has also been used to forecast the thickness of zinc coatings. By using Doehlert design to optimize temperature, withdrawal speed, and dipping (immersion duration), Ben Nasr et al. [31] supported the idea that coating thickness may be reduced without altering the chemical composition of the alloys explained in the ZB. By Jin et al. [33], the density functional theory (DFT) is utilized. The authors determined how different alloys attached to the ZB affected the results. They divided the alloys into two categories: alloys that are effective and alloys that are not. The researchers concluded that while Mg, Ag, and Sn are ineffective alloys that serve purposes other than reducing coating thickness, Ni, V, and Ti are effective alloys that aid to do so [26].

8.2.5 *Energy-Saving Techniques in the HDG Method*

Szymczyk and Kluczek's [34] emphasis was on an emission-free galvanization process and energy savings. They assessed how the galvanization process was progressing at the time, performed a heat balance analysis, and created a thermodynamic transition diagram for the hot-dip galvanization production line. They also research phenomena connected to entropy. The authors lowered energy use by up to 23% by replacing the conventional electric heater with cogeneration technology. Additionally, they claimed that using a cogeneration system effectively reduces energy extraction for the galvanization procedure [34]. Gases like liquified petroleum gas are utilized in conventional electric ovens to heat the zinc bath kettle. Valencia et al.'s [35] investigation into the decrease in petrol consumption during HDG. The researchers implemented an energy management device, looked at energy performance indicators, and realized 3.2% of their prospective savings [35]. Sundaramoorthy et al.'s [4] "enhanced galvanizing energy profiler decision support system (E-GEPDSS)" design was created using the heat balancing method as well. The implementation of each of these strategies resulted in an important reduction in energy losses, according to the authors [4]. Bhadra et al. [36] made use of the GEPDSS design in the galvanizing line and claimed that extending the life of the zinc bath kettle results in significant energy savings from the galvanizing furnace. A formula that calculates the effectiveness of a zinc bath furnace was created by Blakey and Beck [3]. The researchers analyzed the relationship between thermal efficiency and specific usage of energy for both demand and supply and concluded that all these strategies lessen reliance on production rate for energy usage minimization [3].

8.3 Evaluation of Literature Survey

Numerous studies have examined the impact of alloy adding to the zinc bath kettle, according to the literature review. They examined the impact on coating its thickness, surface design, and microstructure in addition to corrosion resistance. Investigators have thoroughly examined and recorded the impact of temperature and immersion time. Although a statistical method for conducting experiments is acknowledged, there are far less publications on the subject than there are for studies on the chemical makeup of zinc bath kettles. Several investigators have also conducted studies based on Industry 4.0 to reduce the use of energy in the HDG method. Figure 8.1 displays a graphic depiction of the source material that has been examined for this essay.

Important details about the HDG method have been analyzed from the literature review and are discussed here. (See Figures 8.2 and 8.3.)

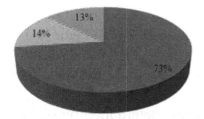

■ Effect of zinc bath alloy, temperature & immersion time
■ Statistical techniques in hot-dip galvanization
■ Energy saving approach in hot-dip galvanization

Figure 8.1   Analyses of the HDG technique's material.

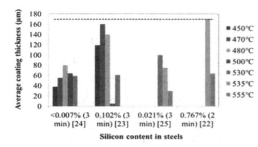

Figure 8.2   For varied levels of silicon contained in steels, the impact of temperature on zinc coating thickness is seen.

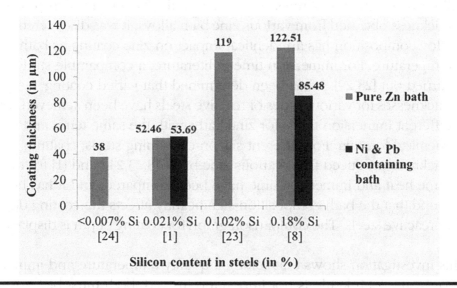

Figure 8.3   Coating thickness measured after three minutes of immersion in a variety of 450°C galvanizing baths for metals including silicon.

- It has been discovered that the ZB kettle or its associated parameters have a stronger impact on the attributes of ZC, including coating thickness, corrosion resistance, Rockwell hardness, or microframework.
- The internal temperature of the ZB kettle, the length of immersion, and the chemical makeup of the alloys in the bath are the three main contributing variables.
- The most troublesome element, aside from the zinc bath kettle, is the material's reactivity. The amount of silicon in the material serves as a proxy for its sensitivity. The coating thickness is more heavily motivated by the reactive steel.
- The spectrum of different reactive steel kinds determined by silicon percentage is indicated in [2]. All these steels exhibit diverse behaviors at various levels of temperature during immersion, and in accordance with the alloy makeup of the zinc bath. Data on coating thickness for a variety of temperatures has been gathered from [22–25] and compared to various silicon-containing steels.
- For the same immersion period of three minutes, LSS (0.021% Si) reached its maximum coating temperature at 530°C [23], while steels with very low silicon content (0.007%) reached their maximum coating temperature at 480°C [24]. Maximum coating for Sandelin steels was achieved at 470°C; these steels exhibit varying coating thickness at temps that vary. For steel with a high silicon content, the greatest coating thickness was achieved at 535°C after two minutes of immersion (0.767%) [22].
- Following a review of the survey [1,2,8] and [10] comparing the coating thickness obtained from various zinc bath alloys, it was discovered that alloy composition has an identical impact on zinc coating as bath temperature. For immersion time in literature, a comparable study is carried out [28,29]. It has been determined that varied coating thicknesses for various types of reactive steels have been achieved with different immersion times for zinc baths with the same temp and chemical formula. For different silicon-containing steels, coating thickness produced from various zinc baths [8,23,24], and [1] for the same heat and immersion time have been compared, and it has been found that the bath composition significantly affects the coating depth of reactive steels. The comparison graph for coating depth is displayed.

This investigation shows that setting a quality temperature and immersion time for a zinc bath kettle is not important; instead, both must be chosen in accordance with the products' chemical makeup and the desired coating thickness. For Industry 4.0, to attain the ideal coating thickness, alloys that would track the reactivity of steels must be stated to the zinc bath making alloys composition if any galvanizing plant's product has a higher-than-average silicon content (for instance, more than 75%).

8.4 Research Gap and Scope for Future Research

A few investigators have created works of literature inspired by Industry 4.0 for the use of design experiments and energy-saving. Even though there have been few researchers on the impact of temperature and the addition of zinc bath alloy on different galvanized product qualities, the conclusions from these studies have not been statistically validated. In this area, the experimental approach is still only occasionally and inconsistently used. Several studies, including [5–7,26,31,32], and [37], have focused on the use of statistical approaches, such as the planning of tests in the galvanizing unit and to examine the behavior of variables. However, the use of a statistical instrument like DOE for reducing energy consumption is lacking. Some ways have been used by the researcher to minimize the use of energy, including energy management systems [34], thermodynamic approaches, and cogeneration of heat [35].

Future research on Industry 4.0 and the galvanization procedure should examine statistical methods. The DOE provides a fair estimate and data that has been verified statistically. Since DOE distributes experimental data, using information from energizing industries and doing case studies would help to define the necessity for testing or shorten the time required for it. Future research may examine the merged impact of zinc bath alloys, temperatures, and immersion time on different reactive steel types utilizing statistical methodologies like different DOE components. Additionally, the optimization of energy use using the DOE tool may prove to be a significant field for future study.

8.5 Conclusion

The goal of this literature survey is to examine how galvanizing firms use DOE tools and energy-saving techniques in HDG operation and to comprehend how various HDG-related elements behave for Industry 4.0. The following conclusions have been reached based on the literature review:

- The paucity of industrial information and use of statistical methods like DOE regarding the galvanization method have been noted. Many authors have employed statistical software like DOE. Most of the literature is based on experimental findings for a certain kind of steel sample and galvanizing conditions.

- A small number of researchers use the energy-saving strategy in HDG to conserve the gas and electricity used to heat the zinc bath furnace.
- The most problematic aspects of the HDG process have been identified as excessive reactive steel coating thickness, power failures from the zinc bath furnace, and a decrease in corrosion resistance. These three problems are linked to one another. In addition to using more energy and zinc, a thicker coating raises the cost of galvanizing. Deterioration of the coating's look and corrosion resistance further raises the likelihood that customers may reject the goods. The primary variables that significantly affect coating thickness and other coating attributes including corrosion resistance and surface attractiveness are the zinc bath alloys, immersion time, immersion temperature, and amount of silicon contained in the steel sample.
- Depending on the level of each element, all these parameters can have either good or negative impact on galvanizing characteristics. To enhance the HDG process, every component must be present at its ideal level. When all factors pertaining to the galvanization procedure are taken into consideration, it is discovered that case research depends on the use of statistical techniques in the galvanizing firms is necessary, which aids in understanding the practical implications that result from the galvanization procedure.
- The use of statistical sources and procedures results in a statistically important and validated outcome that keeps power, contributes to the improvement of the quality of goods, and is also beneficial to the galvanizing industries.

References

1. Kania, H., Saternus, M., and Kudláček, J. (2020). Structural aspects of decreasing the corrosion resistance of zinc coating obtained in baths with Al, Ni, and Pb additives. *Materials, 13*(2), 385.
2. Kania, H., Mendala, J., Kozuba, J., and Saternus, M. (2020). Development of bath chemical composition for batch hot-dip galvanizing—A review. *Materials, 13*(18), 4168.

3. Blakey, S. G., and Beck, S. B. M. (2004). Energy consumption and capacity utilization of galvanizing furnaces. *Proceedings of the Institution of Mechanical Engineers, Part E: Journal of Process Mechanical Engineering, 218*(4), 251–259.

4. Sundaramoorthy, S., Phuong, Q., Gopalakrishnan, B., and Latif, H. H. (2016). Heat balance analysis of annealing furnaces and zinc pot in continuous hot dip galvanizing lines. *Energy Engineering, 113*(2), 12–47.

5. Wang, Y. (2018). Study on influence factors of zinc layer thickness via response surface method, Taguchi method and genetic algorithm. *Ind. Eng. Manag, 7*(1000245), 2169-0316.

6. Shukla, S. K., Sadhukhan, A. K., and Gupta, P. (2017). Development of ANN model for prediction of coating thickness in hot dip galvanizing process. *Int. J. Mater. Sci. Eng., 5*, 60–68.

7. Fernandes, L. S., de Figueiredo, J. D. L., de Araújo Filho, O. O., and de Araújo, E. G. (2019). Blocking of factorial experiments in galvanized wire zinc weight test. *Journal of Materials Research and Technology, 8*(1), 871–875.

8. Kania, H., and Komorowski, L. (2016). The influence of the chemical composition of a zinc bath upon corrosion resistance of coatings obtained on sebisty steel. *Solid State Phenomena, 246*, 85–90.

9. Kania, H., and Liberski, P. (2014). Synergistic influence of the addition of Al, Ni and Pb to a zinc bath upon growth kinetics and structure of coatings. *Solid State Phenomena, 212*, 115–120.

10. Kania, H., Saternus, M., Kudláček, J., and Svoboda, J. (2020). Microstructure characterization and corrosion resistance of zinc coating obtained in a zn-alnibi galvanizing bath. *Coatings, 10*(8), 758.

11. Królikowska, A., Komorowski, L., and Bonora, P. L. (2020). Pitting corrosion of hot-dip galvanized coatings. *Materials, 13*(9), 2031.

12. Shukla, S. K., Deepa, M., and Kumar, S. (2012). Effect of Mg addition (in zinc bath) on galvanized sheet quality. *International Journal of Materials Engineering, 2*(6), 105–111.

13. Tang, N. Y. (2008). Control of silicon reactivity in general galvanizing. *Journal of Phase Equilibria and Diffusion, 29*(4), 337–344.

14. Saravanan, P., and Srikanth, S. (2018). Surface defects and their control in hot dip galvanized and galvannealed sheets. *International Journal of Advanced Research In Chemical Science (Ijarcs), 5*(11), 11–23.

15. Bondareva, O., and Melnikov, A. A. (2016). Improving the quality of the coating at hot-dip galvanizing of machine steels in the zinc melt with microadditives of nickel. *Key Engineering Materials, 685*, 380–384.

16. Pistofidis, N., Vourlias, G., Konidaris, S., Pavlidou, E., and Stergioudis, G. (2007). The combined effect of nickel and bismuth on the structure of hot-dip zinc coatings. *Materials Letters, 61*(10).

17. Fratesi, R., Ruffini, N., Malavolta, M., and Bellezze, T. (2002). Contemporary use of Ni and Bi in hot-dip galvanizing. *Surface and Coatings Technology, 157*(1), 34–39.

18. Vourlias, G., Pistofidis, N., Stergioudis, G., and Tsipas, D. (2004). The effect of alloying elements on the crystallization behaviour and on the properties of galvanized coatings. *Crystal Research and Technology: Journal of Experimental and Industrial Crystallography*, *39*(1), 23–29.

19. Katiforis, N., and Papadimitriou, G. (1996). Influence of copper, cadmium and tin additions in the galvanizing bath on the structure, thickness and cracking behaviour of the galvanized coatings. *Surface and Coatings Technology*, *78*(1-3), 185–195.

20. Di Cocco, V., Iacoviello, F., and Natali, S. (2014). Damaging micromechanisms in hot-dip galvanizing Zn based coatings. *Theoretical and Applied Fracture Mechanics*, *70*, 91–98.

21. Bondareva, O. (2015). Study of the temperature effect on the structure and thickness of hot-dip zinc coatings on fixing products. *Applied Mechanics and Materials*, *698*, 355–359.

22. Bondareva, O. S., Melnikov, A. A., and Amosov, A. P. (2014). Influence of hot-dip galvanizing temperature on formation of zinc coating on a steel with a high silicon content. *Adv. Environ. Biol*, *8*, 943–948.

23. Wang, J., Tu, H., Peng, B., Wang, X., Yin, F., and Su, X. (2009). The effects of zinc bath temperature on the coating growth behavior of reactive steel. *Materials characterization*, *60*(11), 1276–1279.

24. Bicao, P., Jianhua, W., Xuping, S., Zhi, L., and Fucheng, Y. (2008). Effects of zinc bath temperature on the coatings of hot-dip galvanizing. *Surface and Coatings Technology*, *202*(9), 1785–1788.

25. Verma, A. R. B., and Van Ooij, W. J. (1997). High-temperature batch hot-dip galvanizing. Part 2. Comparison of coatings formed in the temperature range 520–555 C. *Surface and Coatings Technology*, *89*(1-2), 143–150.

26. Luo, Q., Jin, F., Li, Q., Zhang, J. Y., and Chou, K. C. (2013). The mechanism of dross formation during hot-dip Al-Zn alloy coating process. *Journal for Manufacturing Science and Production*, *13*(1-2), 85–89.

27. Tzimas, E., and Papadimitriou, G. (2001). Cracking mechanisms in high temperature hot-dip galvanized coatings. *Surface and Coatings Technology*, *145*(1-3), 176–185.

28. Hakim, A. A., Rajagukguk, T. O., and Sumardi, S. (2018). The effect of immersion time to low carbon steel hardness and microstructure with hot dip galvanizing coating method. In *IOP Conference Series: Materials Science and Engineering* (Vol. 285, No. 1, p. 012019). IOP Publishing.

29. Sepper, S., Peetsalu, P., Kulu, P., Saarna, M., and Mikli, V. (2016). The role of silicon in the hot dip galvanizing process. *Proceedings of the Estonian Academy of Sciences*, *65*(2).

30. Bondareva, O. S., and Melnikov, A. A. (2016, November). Effect of the silicon content in steel on the hot-dip zinc coating microstructure formation. In *IOP Conference Series: Materials Science and Engineering* (Vol. 156, No. 1, p. 012015). IOP Publishing.

31. Snoussi, A., Bradai, C., and Halouani, F. (2008). Optimization of hot-dip galvanizing process of reactive steels: Minimizing zinc consumption without alloy additions. *Materials Letters*, *62*(19), 3328–3330.

32. Michal, P., Gombár, M., Vagaská, A., Piteľ, J., and Kmec, J. (2013). Experimental study and modeling of the zinc coating thickness. *Advanced Materials Research*, *712*, 382–386.

33. Jin, H. M., Li, Y., Liu, H. L., and Wu, P. (2000). Study on the behavior of additives in steel hot-dip galvanizing by DFT calculations. *Chemistry of materials*, *12*(7), 1879–1883.

34. Szymczyka, J., and Kluczekb, A. (2017). Increasing the energy efficiency of a hot-dip galvanizing plant and reducing its environmental impact. *Journal of Power Technologies*, *97*(5), 349–358.

35. Valencia-Ochoa, G., Ramos, E., and Meriño, L. (2017). Energy planning for gas consumption reduction in a hot dip galvanizing plant. *Chemical Engineering Transactions*, *57*, 697–702.

36. Bhadra, S., Gopalakrishnan, B., and Chaudhari, S. (2013, March). Energy efficiency in continuous galvanizing lines. In *2013 International Renewable and Sustainable Energy Conference (IRSEC)* (pp. 361–366). IEEE.

37. Smith, J. R., and Larson, C. (2019). Statistical approaches in surface finishing. Part 3. Design-of-experiments. *Transactions of the IMF*, *97*(6), 289–294.

Chapter 9

Phase Change Materials for Enhancing Heat Transfer in Latent Heat Storage Systems

Agnivesh Kumar Sinha[1], Harendra Kumar Narang[2],
Somnath Bhattacharya[2], Ram Krishna Rathore[1],
Nitin Upadhyay[3], Gulab Pamnani[4], and Shashikant Verma[5]

[1]*Mechanical Engineering Department, Rungta College of Engineering and Technology, Bhilai, Chhattisgarh*
[2]*Department of Mechanical Engineering, National Institute of Technology Raipur, Chhattisgarh*
[3]*Department of Mechanical Engineering, Madhav Institute of Technology & Science Gwalior, Madhya Pradesh*
[4]*Department of Mechanical Engineering, Malaviya National Institute of Technology Jaipur, Rajasthan*
[5]*Department of Mechanical Engineering, National Institute of Technology, Durgapur, West Bengal*

9.1 Introduction

Energy is the key to the development and advancement of any nation. Demands for energy have been increasing at a very rapid rate. This huge demand for energy is fulfilled mostly by the exploitation of fossil fuels. This results in harmful emissions and thus increases the overall carbon footprint of energy. For this purpose, several nations have made sincere attempts for reducing the emission and carbon footprint by generation of energy. Harnessing energy from renewable sources is one of the ways to produce

DOI: 10.4324/9781003439684-9

clean energy with less of a carbon footprint. But there are challenges like high initial cost, low efficiency of energy conversion, and intermittent energy delivery, which are some of the hurdles in the way of generating cleaner energy from renewable sources like sun, wind, etc. Therefore, thermal energy storage (TES) became one of the best alternative solutions for the energy generated from fossil fuels. However, low charging and discharging attributes of phase change materials (PCM) are still a challenge in latent heat energy storage systems.[1]

Research shows that solidification time is higher than the melting time of PCM in thermal energy storage systems.[2] This occurs due to lower value of heat transfer coefficient of PCM during the solidification process. Researchers have employed encapsulation techniques to improve the heat transfer capabilities of PCM and to increase the thermal efficiency of thermal energy storage systems.[3] Encapsulation is a remedy to deal with the PCM having low thermal conductivity. Encapsulation increases the surface area for heat transfer, which further improves the efficiency of thermal energy storage systems. Heat transfer capabilities can also be enhanced by the incorporation of nano-sized dispersoids. Researchers have utilized nano-particles of graphene in PCM for enhancing the thermal conductivity and the rate of energy storage rate of PCM.[4] PCM also prevents PCM leakage during phase change in TES systems. Graphene aerogel was also used for changing PCM into phase change composites for enhancing the thermal conductivity and heat transfer performance of PCM.[5] Heat transfer efficiency of TEM depends on the thermo-physical properties of PCM. Thermal conductivity, latent heat, specific heat capacity, phase change temperature in desired range of operation, etc., are some of the key attributes of PCM that govern the heat transfer in latent heat TES systems.[6]

The influence of Industry 4.0 on the sustainability of energy has always been a concern for the research community. A study manifested a model for supporting the development of a sustainable renewable energy supply chain as per Industry 4.0.[7] Research has been conducted to optimize the energy produced from renewable sources using Industry 4.0.[8] Further, possibility of application of artificial intelligence for energy storage systems was determined by researchers to assess the impact of Industry 4.0 on improved performance of systems.[9]

This review deals with the modifications of PCM for enhancing the heat transfer in latent heat energy storage systems based on encapsulation and incorporation of nano-particles, dispersoids as reinforcement in PCM composites. The effect of these modifications on thermo-physical attributes of various PCM is observed and analyzed. This review also unveils the key research gaps pertinent to this domain.

9.2 Phase Change Materials (PCM)

PCM play a key role in latent heat energy storage systems. Latent heat is stored in PCM during change of phase. When PCM absorbs heat energy, phase changes from solid to liquid at a constant temperature, and when it rejects heat, the phase of PCM changes from liquid to solid at a constant temperature, which is termed charging and discharging of PCM, respectively. PCM are classified into three broad categories, namely, organic, inorganic, and eutectics, as shown in Figure 9.1. Paraffins, fatty acids, and organic mixtures are three groups of organic PCM. Inorganic PCM are usually composed of salt hydrates and metallic compounds. In general, inorganic PCM exhibits better thermal conductivity than organic PCM.[10] Eutectic-type PCM consists of two or more different types of PCM. LiOH-KOH is an example of eutectic PCM. Here, both constituent PCMs change their phase at the same time while melting or freezing.

Fatty acids like Capric and myristic acids were used as eutectic PCM in TES system in research.[11] Results showed that PCM exhibits good thermal storage capability. However, it was also reported that PCM manifested poor thermal conductivity, which is a critical attribute of PCM to be used in latent heat energy storage systems. Paraffin wax is the most commonly used PCM in latent heat energy storage systems by researchers.[12,13] Alumina (Al_2O_3) nano-particles[14] were incorporated in paraffin wax (PCM) to improve the thermal conductivity of PCM. Higher thermal conductivity of PCM helps in reducing the charging time. Similarly, the thermal performance of fatty acid PCM was enhanced by the addition of graphene nano-particles.[15] Encapsulation of PCM is another way for enhancing the heat transfer capabilities of PCM.[10] Several researchers have studied and reported the effect of encapsulation[16,17] of PCM on the thermal characteristics of latent heat energy storage systems.

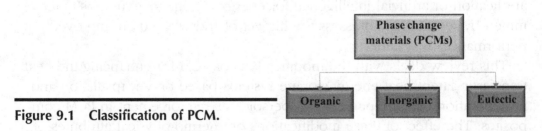

Figure 9.1 Classification of PCM.

9.3 Heat Transfer Enhancement by Modification of PCM

In latent heat energy storage systems, heat transfer performance of PCM is of vital importance. Heat transfer performance of PCM depends on the thermo-physical properties of PCM like density, melting/freezing temperature, latent heat, thermal conductivity. Moreover, it is also reported that encapsulation and incorporation of nano-particles or reinforcements in PCM could be beneficial in improving the thermo-physical characteristics of PCM and hence the heat transfer performance of PCM. Table 9.1 shows the thermo-physical properties of various PCM used in TES systems.

9.3.1 *Encapsulation of PCM*

Encapsulation of PCM is the method to improve the heat transfer characteristics of PCM in TES systems. This also eradicates the chances of PCM coming in contact with environment that may lead to corrosion and deterioration in thermal attributes of PCM. Moreover, in the case of eutectic PCM, encapsulation reduces the problems of phase separation in latent heat energy storage systems. Encapsulation of PCM is usually achieved by providing a metallic shell (outer cover) to PCM, which facilitates better heat transfer due to higher surface area of PCM after encapsulation. Also, encapsulation is divided into three sub-categories on the basis of the size of encapsulation, namely, micro-encapsulation, macro-encapsulation, and nano-encapsulation.

Researchers have employed encapsulation in TES wherein hybrid PCM was enveloped in a capsule.[18] Results manifested reduction in discharging time of PCM, which was facilitated by the small size and high shell thickness of the capsule. In other research, alumina shell was utilized to encapsulate Al-Si based PCM, which resulted in improving the heat transfer rate.[19] Studies also showed that 90.2% and 98.3% were the discharging and charging efficiency of the TES system, respectively. Wood-based PCM was encapsulated by polymer (poly melamine-urea-formaldehyde) in research where Cu was deposited at the inner surface of lumen of wood.[20] This helped in achieving the improved shape and thermal stability. Moreover, it was also observed that metallic wood-based PCM exhibited better thermal conductivity (300%) than raw wood. Similarly, closed cell Poly HIPE (high internal phase emulsion) monolith was used to encapsulate octadecane paraffin, which manifested outstanding usability (tested up to 100 cycles of heating and cooling).[17] This also resulted in raising the melting temperature of PCM by 3°C and reduced solidification temperature by 1°C. For the purpose of comparison, researchers have carried

Table 9.1 Thermo-Physical Properties of PCM

PCM	Encapsulation Shell	Density (Kg/m^3)	Melting/Freezing Temperature (K)	Latent heat (KJ/Kg)	Thermal conductivity (W/m K)	References
Paraffin	–	805	333	120	0.22	18
Al-25%Si	Al_2O_3	1.91×10^3	850	127.1	2.35	19
n-octadecane	Melamine-urea-formaldehyde polymer	–	303	95.5	0.23	20
Paraffin wax A53 doped with graphene	–	806	325	170	0.78	21
Granulated Paraffin wax	–	861	334	213	0.4	22
Multi-walled carbon nanotube enhanced n-octadecane	–	–	842.8	217	0.67	23
Octadecanol	–	812	322	234	0.23	24
Acetamide	–	1159	355	263	–	25
Octadecane	pentaerythritol tetra poly (ethylene glycol) diacrylate	0.68	334	210	0.21	17
Paraffin wax	nano-Si_3N_4	–	332	100.4	0.35	12
Paraffin wax with CuO-Multi-walled carbon nano tubes	–	958.3	333	–	0.25	26

out thermo-physical characterization of bulk and macro-encapsulated paraffin wax.[27] Macro-encapsulation resulted in reducing the charging time up to 80% when compared to bulk PCM. Research has also been carried out for numerically analyzing the thermal characteristics of PCM (paraffin wax) encapsulated latent heat energy storage systems.[2]

Latent heat energy storage tanks design for building used for heating was improved by researchers by encapsulating paraffin wax PCM in water, which led to the improvement in heat storage capacity and energy density of TES system.[28] Shape of capsule also play an important role in deciding the heat transfer performance of TES system. A research manifested that ellipsoidal capsule[3] took 60% lesser time for discharging of PCM when compared to conventional cylindrical capsule. However, this reduction in discharging time of PCM was achieved at the cost of energy density, which was lower than that of conventional cylindrical capsules.

9.3.2 *Incorporation of Nano-Particles in PCM*

Besides encapsulation, another way of enhancing the heat transfer efficiency in a TES system is the addition of nano-particles or inclusion of nano-sized reinforcements. This leads to improvement in thermo-physical attributes of PCM. Researchers have utilized nano-Al_2O_3 in doping shells of encapsulated n-hexadecane (PCM), which resulted in increasing the thermal conductivity of PCM and hence the overall heat transfer efficiency of the TES system.[29] Results also showed that the nano-particles doped PCM exhibited good thermal recycling stability. Nano-SiO_2 was also used as matrix wherein a eutectic mixture of myristic and capric acid was used as PCM in the form of composites in the TES system.[11] Incorporation of nano-particles in PCM enhanced its thermal stability and thermal conductivity. Paraffinic films with polyamide foams were also used with SiC and BN nano-particle reinforcements, which led to improvement in thermal stability of PCM in TES.[30] Incorporation of Nano-Si_3N_4 in paraffin wax PCM resulted in increasing the thermal conductivity of the paraffin wax.[12]

Researchers have also investigated the effect of adding copper nano-particles in paraffin wax (PCM), where it was inferred that the melting time of nano-enhanced PCM reduced significantly by 19%.[31] Research was also carried out to investigate the thermal behavior of paraffin wax (PCM) doped with nano alumina via simulation.[14] Results revealed that incorporation of nano-particles in paraffin wax increases the density and thermal conductivity. This research was beneficial in determining the optimum composition of nano-particles in PCM for maximum heat transfer in TES system. Nano-enhanced PCM usually showed improvement in their properties, like thermal conductivity and thermal stability, etc. And graphene-based PCM have their potential applications in automobile and aerospace industries.[15]

9.4 Conclusions and Future Trends

This review disseminates brief information on the heat transfer enhancement in latent heat storage systems. Two ways of enhancing heat transfer performance in TES, namely, encapsulation and incorporation of nano-particles in PCM, are discussed and analyzed. Researchers have utilized nano-particles of carbon (graphene), Si_3N_4, SiC, BN, SiO_2, Al_2O_3, Cu, etc. However, limited research has been reported on incorporation of nano-particles of Ag, ZrO_2, Al, Fe_3O_4, TiO_2, Fe_2O_3, ZnO, and Y_2O_3 in PCM for improvement in heat transfer capabilities and other thermo-physical attributes like thermal conductivity, density, melting point, and heat of fusion. Several studies have also reported improvement in thermal stability of TES due to encapsulation and the addition of nano-particles. Literature also showed that there is a scarcity of research on encapsulation of PCM for enhancing heat transfer performance of TES. Also, research on the use of polymers for encapsulation is limited. And there is scarcity of research on shape optimization of capsules for maximizing heat transfer.

The literature shows that the use of encapsulation of PCM and the addition of nano-particles in PCM often results in reducing the discharging time along with charging time of PCM in TES, which is sometimes not desirable. This also limits the application of enhanced PCM in latent heat energy storage systems used for heating.

Funding

This research did not receive any specific grant from funding agencies in the public, commercial, or not-for-profit sectors.

Compliance with Ethical Standards

The authors declare that there is no conflict of interest.

Acknowledgments

Authors are thankful to Rungta College of Engineering and Technology, Bhilai for providing the platform for this research.

References

1. Khan, Z., Khan, Z., & Ghafoor, A. (2016). A review of performance enhancement of PCM based latent heat storage system within the context of materials, thermal stability and compatibility. In *Energy Conversion and Management* (Vol. 115, pp. 132–158). Elsevier Ltd. 10.1016/j.enconman.2016.02.045

2. Felix Regin, A., Solanki, S. C., & Saini, J. S. (2009). An analysis of a packed bed latent heat thermal energy storage system using PCM capsules: Numerical investigation. *Renewable Energy, 34*(7), 1765–1773. 10.1016/j.renene.2008.12.012

3. Xu, T., Humire, E. N., Trevisan, S., Ignatowicz, M., Sawalha, S., & Chiu, J. N. (2022). Experimental and numerical investigation of a latent heat thermal energy storage unit with ellipsoidal macro-encapsulation. *Energy, 238.* 10.1016/j.energy.2021.121828

4. Mayilvelnathan, V., & Valan Arasu, A. (2020). Experimental investigation on thermal behavior of graphene dispersed erythritol PCM in a shell and helical tube latent energy storage system. *International Journal of Thermal Sciences, 155.* 10.1016/j.ijthermalsci.2020.106446

5. Kashyap, S., Kabra, S., & Kandasubramanian, B. (2020). Graphene aerogel-based phase changing composites for thermal energy storage systems. In *Journal of Materials Science* (Vol. 55, Issue 10, pp. 4127–4156). Springer. 10.1007/s10853-019-04325-7

6. Soares, N., Costa, J. J., Gaspar, A. R., & Santos, P. (2013). Review of passive PCM latent heat thermal energy storage systems towards buildings' energy efficiency. In *Energy and Buildings* (Vol. 59, pp. 82–103). 10.1016/j.enbuild.2012.12.042

7. Mastrocinque, E., Ramírez, F. J., Honrubia-Escribano, A., & Pham, D. T. (2022). Industry 4.0 enabling sustainable supply chain development in the renewable energy sector: A multi-criteria intelligent approach. *Technological Forecasting and Social Change, 182.* 10.1016/j.techfore.2022.121813

8. Pandey, V., Sircar, A., Bist, N., Solanki, K., & Yadav, K. (2023). Accelerating the renewable energy sector through Industry 4.0: Optimization opportunities in the digital revolution. *International Journal of Innovation Studies.* 10.1016/j.ijis.2023.03.003

9. Ahmad, T., Zhu, H., Zhang, D., Tariq, R., Bassam, A., Ullah, F., AlGhamdi, A. S., & Alshamrani, S. S. (2022). Energetics Systems and artificial intelligence: Applications of industry 4.0. In *Energy Reports* (Vol. 8, pp. 334–361). Elsevier Ltd. 10.1016/j.egyr.2021.11.256

10. Jouhara, H., Żabnieńska-Góra, A., Khordehgah, N., Ahmad, D., & Lipinski, T. (2020). Latent thermal energy storage technologies and applications: A review. *International Journal of Thermofluids, 5–6.* 10.1016/j.ijft.2020.100039

11. Meng, D., Zhao, K., Zhao, W., & Jiang, G. (2017). Preparation and characterization of CA-MA eutectic/silicon dioxide nanoscale composite phase change material from water glass via sol-gel method. *Journal Wuhan University of Technology, Materials Science Edition, 32*(5), 1048–1056. 10.1007/s11595-017-1709-4

12. Sun, N., & Xiao, Z. (2016). Paraffin wax-based phase change microencapsulation embedded with silicon nitride nanoparticles for thermal energy storage. *Journal of Materials Science, 51*(18), 8550–8561. 10.1007/s10853-016-0116-0

13. Sharma, H. K., Verma, S. K., Singh, P. K., Kumar, S., Paswan, M. K., & Singhal, P. (2019). Performance analysis of paraffin wax as PCM by using hybrid zinc-cobalt-iron oxide nano-fluid on latent heat energy storage system. *Materials Today: Proceedings, 26,* 1461–1464. 10.1016/j.matpr.2020.02.300

14. Teja, P. N. S., Gugulothu, S. K., Sastry, G. R., Burra, B., & Bhurat, S. S. (2021). Numerical analysis of nanomaterial-based sustainable latent heat thermal energy storage system by improving thermal characteristics of phase change material. *Environmental Science and Pollution Research.* 10.1007/s11356-021-15485-y

15. Nagar, S., & Sharma, K. (2021). Modern solar systems driven by nanoparticles-based fatty acids and paraffin wax phase change materials. In *Journal of Materials Science* (Vol. 56, Issue 8, pp. 4941–4966). Springer. 10.1007/s10853-020-05575-6

16. Mohaghegh, M. R., Alomair, Y., Alomair, M., Tasnim, S. H., Mahmud, S., & Abdullah, H. (2021). Melting of PCM inside a novel encapsulation design for thermal energy storage system. *Energy Conversion and Management: X, 11.* 10.1016/j.ecmx.2021.100098

17. Zhang, T., Xu, Z., Li, X., Gao, G., & Zhao, Y. (2020). Closed-cell, phase change material-encapsulated, emulsion-templated monoliths for latent heat storage: Flexibility and rapid preparation. *Applied Materials Today, 21.* 10.1016/j.apmt.2020.100831

18. Baruah, J. S., Athawale, V., Rath, P., & Bhattacharya, A. (2022). Melting and energy storage characteristics of macro-encapsulated PCM-metal foam system. *International Journal of Heat and Mass Transfer, 182.* 10.1016/j.ijheatmasstransfer.2021.121993

19. Koide, H., Kurniawan, A., Takahashi, T., Kawaguchi, T., Sakai, H., Sato, Y., Chiu, J. N., & Nomura, T. (2022). Performance analysis of packed bed latent heat storage system for high-temperature thermal energy storage using pellets composed of micro-encapsulated phase change material. *Energy, 238.* 10.1016/j.energy.2021.121746

20. Lin, X., Chen, X., Weng, L., Hu, D., Qiu, C., Liu, P., Zhang, Y., Fan, M., Sun, W., & Guo, X. (2022). In-situ copper ion reduction and micro encapsulation of wood-based composite PCM with effective anisotropic thermal conductivity and energy storage. *Solar Energy Materials and Solar Cells, 242,* 111762. 10.1016/j.solmat.2022.111762

21. Pássaro, J., Rebola, A., Coelho, L., Conde, J., Evangelakis, G. A., Prouskas, C., Papageorgiou, D. G., Zisopoulou, A., & Lagaris, I. E. (2022). Effect of fins and nanoparticles in the discharge performance of PCM thermal storage system with a multi pass finned tube heat exchange. *Applied Thermal Engineering*, *212*, 118569. 10.1016/j.applthermaleng.2022.118569

22. Surya, A., Nallusamy, N., Shreyas, Vishnu, B., & Girish, R. (2022). Comparative study of heat transfer enhancement in a latent heat thermal energy storage system using mild steel and stainless steel spherical PCM containers. *Materials Today: Proceedings*. 10.1016/j.matpr.2022.03.568

23. Gupta, A. K., Mishra, G., & Singh, S. (2022). Numerical study of MWCNT enhanced PCM melting through a heated undulated wall in the latent heat storage unit. *Thermal Science and Engineering Progress*, *27*. 10.1016/j.tsep.2021.101172

24. Park, J., Shin, D. H., Shin, Y., & Karng, S. W. (2019). Analysis of heat transfer in latent heat thermal energy storage using a flexible PCM container. *Heat and Mass Transfer/Waerme- Und Stoffuebertragung*, *55*(6), 1571–1581. 10.1007/s00231-018-02534-5

25. Abu-Hamdeh, N. H., & Alnefaie, K. A. (2019). Assessment of thermal performance of PCM in latent heat storage system for different applications. *Solar Energy*, *177*, 317–323. 10.1016/j.solener.2018.11.035

26. Kalbande, V. P., Fating, G., Mohan, M., Rambhad, K., & Sinha, A. K. (2022). Experimental and theoretical study for suitability of hybrid nano enhanced phase change material for thermal energy storage applications. *Journal of Energy Storage*, *51*. 10.1016/j.est.2022.104431

27. Hu, M. H., Xu, T., & Chiu, J. N. (2022). Experimental analysis of submerged coil and encapsulated slab latent heat storage. *Applied Thermal Engineering*, *209*. 10.1016/j.applthermaleng.2022.118259

28. Koželj, R., Mlakar, U., Zavrl, E., Stritih, U., & Stropnik, R. (2021). An experimental and numerical analysis of an improved thermal storage tank with encapsulated PCM for use in retrofitted buildings for heating. *Energy and Buildings*, *248*. 10.1016/j.enbuild.2021.111196

29. Wei, S., Duan, Z., Xia, Y., Huang, C., Ji, R., Zhang, H., Xu, F., Sun, L., & Sun, Y. (2019). Preparation and thermal performances of microencapsulated phase change materials with a nano-Al2O3-doped shell. *Journal of Thermal Analysis and Calorimetry*, *138*(1), 233–241. 10.1007/s10973-019-08097-9

30. Clausi, M., Zahid, M., Shayganpour, A., & Bayer, I. S. (2022). Polyimide foam composites with nano-boron nitride (BN) and silicon carbide (SiC) for latent heat storage. *Advanced Composites and Hybrid Materials*. 10.1007/s42114-022-00426-1

31. Du, R., Li, W., Xiong, T., Yang, X., Wang, Y., & Shah, K. W. (2019). Numerical investigation on the melting of nanoparticle-enhanced PCM in latent heat energy storage unit with spiral coil heat exchanger. *Building Simulation*, *12*(5), 869–879. 10.1007/s12273-019-0527-3

Chapter 10

A Sustainable Green Manufacturing in the Era of Industry 4.0: Possibilities and Challenges

Manish RK Sahu[1], Naveen Jain[1], and Ajay Tripathi[2]

[1]Shri Shankaracharya institute of professional management and Technology, Raipur
[2]New Government Engineering College, Raipur

10.1 Introduction

The transition to Industry 4.0 is characterized by the integration of cyber-physical systems, the Internet of Things (IoT), big data analytics, and artificial intelligence into manufacturing processes. The term "Industry 4.0" or "the Fourth Industrial Revolution" is frequently used to describe this new organizational level of economical development. The main concept of Industry 4.0 aims to leverage future technology in a way that closely integrates technical and business processes ensuring that manufacturing runs with continual high quality and low cost in a flexible, efficient, and sustainable manner (Ansari et al., 2013). Concurrently, concerns about environmental sustainability and resource efficiency have gained momentum. This chapter addresses the potential alignment between these two trends, focusing on how Industry 4.0 technologies can enable and enhance sustainable green manufacturing practices. A growing degree of digitization in the last 20 years has altered

DOI: 10.4324/9781003439684-10

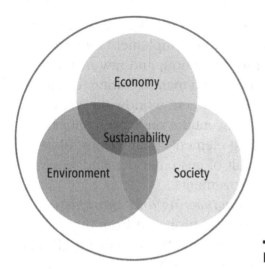

Figure 10.1   The three pillars of sustainability.

industrial production systems, resulting in an intelligent, networked, and decentralized manufacturing. According to the well-known triple bottom line (TBL) sustainability conceptualization (shown in Figure 10.1), a company would be able to achieve sustainable results provided it is capable of simultaneously improving environmental, social, and economic performances. Various companies from the west are urged to become more proactive regarding their environmental and social stance and move toward more sustainable manufacturing practices. In this vein, researchers have started to think about lean manufacturing with a renewed interest in creating greener solutions capable not only of minimizing wastes but also of reducing, by extending, moderating, and updating lean methodologies, the adverse effects of the traditionally employed industrial practices on the environment and social systems.

10.2   Basic Terminology and Conceptual Framing

10.2.1   Sustainable Green Manufacturing

This section provides an overview of sustainable green manufacturing principles, including waste reduction, energy efficiency, eco-friendly materials, and circular economy concepts. The importance of these practices in mitigating environmental impacts and achieving long-term industrial sustainability is discussed.

In the 1990s, the idea of "green manufacturing" first emerged in the global forum. Fiksel (1996) argued that companies should implement reuse and recycling practices in order to reduce waste, pollution, and raw material consumption. Businesses need to implement green manufacturing techniques if they want to gain a competitive edge and compete worldwide. Various studies emphasized that companies must concentrate on waste control in manufacturing by removing the contributing elements. Many firms adopted environmentally friendly practices as a result of customer demand, environmental protection laws, and technical improvements.

The *International Journal of Precision Engineering and Manufacturing-Green Technology* (IJPEM-GT) was founded and broke off from the *International Journal of Precision Engineering and Manufacturing* (IJPEM) to promote knowledge exchange and teamwork among scholars studying "green manufacturing." The journal's five primary topics were chosen to highlight important issues in energy-environment resource saving based on manufacturing technology:

1. Waste reduction and energy conservation in manufacturing processes
2. Creation of new and renewable energy technologies
3. Developing and producing green products
4. Resources for sustainable manufacturing
5. Sustainable manufacturing management and policy

The International Symposium on Green Manufacturing and Applications (ISGMA) series, which took place in Seoul (2011), Jeju Island (2012), and Hawaii (2013), provided a summary of these subjects and important parameters in order to show the viability of the green manufacturing.

The important influential key parameters of sustainable green manufacturing are shown in Figure 10.2.

From Figure 10.1, we can easily understand the significance of green manufacturing in the era of Industry 4.0. For a better future, it is very important for the society, government industry people, and the general public to be aware of the concepts of green manufacturing and Industry 4.0.

10.2.2 Industry 4.0 Technologies

In this section, a brief exploration of the key technologies underpinning Industry 4.0 is presented. This includes cyber-physical systems, IoT devices, cloud computing, big data analytics, artificial intelligence, and additive

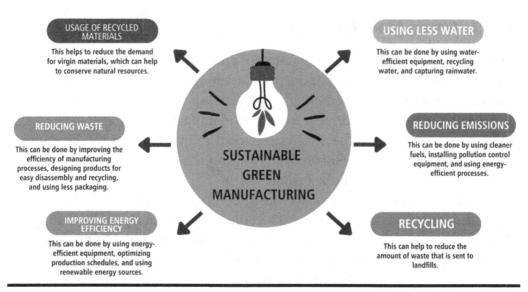

Figure 10.2 The key parameters of sustainable green manufacturing.

manufacturing. The transformative potential of these technologies in optimizing manufacturing processes and enabling data-driven decision making is highlighted. The twenty-first century is marked by the convergence of technological advances under the umbrella term "Industry 4.0," encompassing concepts like the Internet of Things (IoT), big data, artificial intelligence (AI), fuzzy interference system (FIS), and machine learning. These advances present significant opportunities for industries worldwide to reform their traditional manufacturing processes toward more sustainable and efficient ones. (See Figure 10.3.)

We must comprehend the technologies of Industry 4.0, and these technologies are very important for a nation's economical and sustainable development.

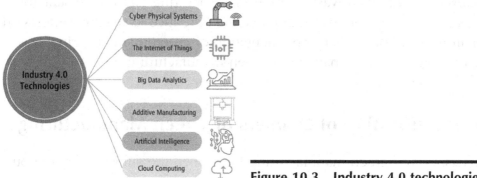

Figure 10.3 Industry 4.0 technologies.

10.2.3 Green Manufacturing Exercises

In order to present a distinct assessment of green manufacturing techniques, a review of the literature was conducted. Green manufacturing, criteria for assessing a system's environmental effectiveness, important success elements for green manufacturing, drivers for green manufacturing, and hurdles for green manufacturing are the subjects covered in the study of the literature. The literature review's main objective is to pinpoint the elements that spur the development of green manufacturing.

The following is a review of various green manufacturing (GM)–related theoretical and empirical literature. The amount of literature on the subject of GM practice is insufficient. There aren't many published works on green manufacturing in its contemporary setting (Deif, 2011). There are other terms used to describe GM, including "environmentally friendly manufacturing," "sustainable manufacturing," "sustainable production," "clean manufacturing," and others. Green production reduces the harmful effects of manufacturing on the environment (Azapagic and Perdan, 2000). Resource usage across the entire product life cycle is taken into account by such an advanced manufacturing system. It balances social and economic advantages without endangering the environment. Through superior process design, product development, and manufacturing operations, it seeks to reduce environmental impact (Deif, 2011). Green manufacturing integrates a number of issues to reduce harmful effects on the environment. It emphasizes the creation of innovative technologies for the transformation of materials without the release of potentially dangerous gases, does away with the usage of toxic or exhaustible materials, and prevents the production of trash (Büyüközkan and Öztürkcan, 2010). The goal of green manufacturing is to apply sustainability concepts to the industrial sector. By rethinking the current industrial process or system, such a paradigm lowers energy consumption and eliminates environmental waste. Green manufacturing employs sustainable methods in product creation and engineering to reduce its negative effects on the environment. For proper implementation of green manufacturing, it is necessary to identify the enablers of green manufacturing.

10.3 Identification of Enablers of Green Manufacturing

Various aspects of green manufacturing have been the subject of numerous research. Enablers in green manufacturing, environmentally conscious manufacturing, environment and sustainable development, green productivity, green processes, green design, sustainable manufacturing, etc., are some of the subjects covered in the review of literature. The literature review's main goal was to pinpoint key elements that would facilitate an easy transition to green manufacturing. A major change in how corporations create products is being brought about by the implementation of polluter pays principles (De Burgos Jiménez and Cespedes Lorente, 2001). Businesses are employing the life cycle analysis approach to reduce toxic waste as a result of the necessity for efficient waste management. Manufacturers are improving their manufacturing methods to address the difficulties brought on by the growing demand for finite resources. In order to make their operations environmentally friendly, they are also under pressure to transition to renewable resources (Barbara et al., 2012).

A wide range of economic advantages flow from the adoption of green manufacturing. These include reduced tax obligations, cash subsidies, tradeable carbon credits, etc. These financial advantages persuade manufacturers to create innovative green technology and innovate a new culture to the industries. Green manufacturing has recently attracted a lot of attention due to its notion of the various costs associated with the process significantly impacted by product design, recycling, and re-manufacturing (Dem and Singh, 2015).

A sustainable procurement process takes into account non-traditional expenses in addition to traditional ones, such as carbon emission costs and end-of-life disposal costs. Faster adoption of green manufacturing is made possible by suppliers' willingness to invest more. Establishing green supply chain mechanisms requires both knowledge of green manufacturing techniques and a readiness to adopt new technology. By integrating green technology throughout their entire supply chains, manufacturers are lowering their carbon footprints. In order to promote and implement green manufacturing in the age of Industry 4.0, it is essential to evaluate the barriers which are responsible for slowing down the pace of green manufacturing adoption.

10.4 Identification of Various Barriers for the Adoption of Green Manufacturing

The implementation of sustainable green manufacturing within an Industry 4.0 framework is not without challenges. This section discusses barriers such as the initial investment cost of adopting new technologies, interoperability issues, data security and privacy concerns, and the need for a skilled workforce adept in both sustainability and digitization.

The various facets of green manufacturing have been the subject of numerous research.

Critical success criteria for green manufacturing, green productivity, green process, green design, sustainable manufacturing, and green scheduling are the subjects covered in the literature review for identifying hurdles. The review of the literature identified the elements that hinder the adoption of green manufacturing.

Different categories have been used to group these obstacles.

10.4.1 Financial Impediments

A significant amount of capital must be invested in green manufacturing. Businesses are hesitant to participate in green manufacturing due to the uncertainties around the rate of return on capital. It is challenging for manufacturers to get financing since banks are hesitant to fund green initiatives.

10.4.2 Technical Limitations

The requirement to integrate more recent advancements with the current systems creates technological impediments. It is challenging for a corporation to adopt new processes and products due to design complexity and operational rigidity. The transformation is made more challenging by limited technological and managerial capabilities, increased infrastructure needs, and the demand to incorporate modern technologies, materials, and processes.

10.4.3 Social Limitations

Businesses struggle with a lack of experts with technical knowledge in green manufacturing. Since green manufacturing is still a new paradigm, there is a shortage of skilled professionals. The lack of institutions that can educate, supervise, and mentor professionals in green manufacturing is the reason for this talent shortage. Businesses must put initiatives in place to modify employees' attitudes about embracing new technologies. To increase their dedication to this cause, businesses should train their personnel on environmental challenges. Customer pressure has a direct effect on businesses' actions about their environmental practices.

10.4.4 Operational Hindrances

Setting up a green supply chain management system is difficult since vendors are reluctant to make technology investments in green. This opposition might be brought on by a lack of understanding of the advantages of adopting green manufacturing practices. According to Del Bro and Junquera (2003), disregarding green considerations at the strategic level may result from factors like a lack of faith in the potential benefits, a lack of management commitment, and a sense of being "out of responsibility" with regard to environmental protection.

10.4.5 Environmental Hindrances

Adoption of green manufacturing depends on effective environmental legislation (Baskaya and Avcı Öztürk, 2011). The development of green manufacturing is hampered by the government's incapacity to offer adequate infrastructure, training, consulting, tax incentives, benefits, etc. Businesses are deterred from investing in green manufacturing by an imprecise regulatory policy of financial subsidies and an arbitrary system of issuance of pollution abatement licenses.

10.5 Possibilities and Benefits of Integration of Green Manufacturing and Industry 4.0

This section delves into the possibilities of integrating sustainable green manufacturing practices with Industry 4.0 technologies. The synergy includes real-time monitoring and control of energy consumption, predictive maintenance to reduce waste, optimized supply chain management for resource efficiency, and AI-driven product design for environmental impact reduction. Each possibility is supported by relevant case studies and practical applications. The integration of green manufacturing and Industry 4.0 represents a significant opportunity for businesses to enhance their environmental sustainability while improving operational efficiency and competitiveness. Here are some possibilities and benefits of integrating these two concepts:

10.5.1 Energy Efficiency

Industry 4.0 technologies, such as IoT (Internet of Things) sensors and data analytics, can monitor and optimize energy consumption in real time. This leads to reduced energy waste and lower greenhouse gas emissions, aligning with green manufacturing goals.

10.5.2 Resource Optimization

Smart manufacturing systems can optimize the use of raw materials and resources by predicting demand and adjusting production processes accordingly, reducing waste, and conserving resources.

10.5.3 Predictive Maintenance

Industry 4.0 enables predictive maintenance, which can prevent equipment breakdowns and reduce downtime. This not only improves production efficiency but also extends the life span of machinery and reduces the need for resource-intensive replacements.

10.5.4 Sustainable Supply Chain

Integration with Industry 4.0 allows companies to monitor and optimize their entire supply chain for sustainability. This includes reducing transportation emissions, minimizing excess inventory, and ensuring ethical sourcing of materials.

10.5.5 Circular Economy

Industry 4.0 can facilitate the implementation of circular economy principles by tracking and tracing products and materials throughout their life cycle. This enables better recycling, re-manufacturing, and reuse of products.

10.5.6 Real-Time Environmental Monitoring

IoT sensors can continuously monitor environmental parameters such as air quality, water quality, and emissions. This data can be used to ensure compliance with environmental regulations and proactively address environmental issues.

10.5.7 Green Product Design

Data analytics and simulation tools in Industry 4.0 can aid in designing products with lower environmental impact. This includes selecting eco-friendly materials and optimizing product life cycles.

10.5.8 Customization and Waste Reduction

Industry 4.0 technologies enable mass customization, reducing overproduction, and minimizing excess inventory. This leads to less waste and a smaller environmental footprint.

10.5.9 Compliance and Reporting

Automated data collection and reporting capabilities of Industry 4.0 can streamline the process of complying with environmental regulations and reporting sustainability metrics to stakeholders.

10.5.10 Employee Engagement

The integration of green manufacturing and Industry 4.0 can also engage employees in sustainability efforts. Digital tools can make it easier for employees to contribute ideas and monitor the environmental impact of their work.

10.5.11 Market Advantage

Green manufacturing practices and Industry 4.0 integration can be used as a competitive advantage, appealing to environmentally conscious consumers and investors who prioritize sustainable practices.

10.5.12 Risk Mitigation

By proactively addressing environmental concerns and complying with regulations, businesses can reduce the risk of fines, legal issues, and damage to their reputation.

To successfully integrate green manufacturing and Industry 4.0, organizations need to develop a comprehensive strategy, invest in the necessary technology and training, and establish a culture of sustainability throughout the company. Collaboration with suppliers and partners is also crucial to extend green practices across the entire value chain.

Detailing the potential benefits of integrating sustainable green manufacturing with Industry 4.0, this section outlines how such an integration can lead to reduced carbon footprints, improved resource utilization, enhanced product quality, and increased competitiveness for manufacturers. Economic, environmental, and social advantages are explored. (See Figures 10.4 and 10.5.)

Figure 10.4   Benefits of sustainable green manufacturing from the economics perspective.

Figure 10.5   Benefits of sustainable green manufacturing from the environmental perspective.

10.6 Future Directions

The study concludes with insights into the future direction of sustainable green manufacturing in the context of Industry 4.0. This includes the potential for further innovation, policy implications, and the role of research and development in addressing emerging challenges.

10.7 Summary and Conclusion

A review of the literature was done to give a comprehensive analysis of the problems with green manufacturing. Additionally, a review of the literature on various approaches used in the current study is done. The numerous measures for evaluating a system's environmental performance, as well as key success factors, drivers, and hurdles for green manufacturing, were determined on the basis of the literature. The literature review's main objective was to pinpoint the elements that spur the development of green manufacturing. Summarizing the key findings, this section emphasizes the transformative potential of integrating sustainable green manufacturing with Industry 4.0 technologies. It underscores the importance of collaboration among industries, academia, and policymakers to drive forward this agenda and ensure a harmonious coexistence of technological progress and environmental responsibility.

References

Ansari, Md. F., Ravinder K.K., Sunil L., Shimi, S.L. and Chatterji, S., (2013), "Analysis of barriers to implement solar power installations in India using interpretive structural modeling technique". Renewable and Sustainable Energy Reviews, 27, pp.163–174.

Azapagic, A., and Perdan, S. (2000), "Indicators of sustainable development for industry: A general framework". Process Safety and Environmental Protection, 78, pp.243–261.

Barbara, L., Yu-Chu, H., David, D. (2012), "Establishing greener products and manufacturing processes". International Journal of Precision Engineering and Manufacturing, 13(7), pp.1029–1036.

Baskaya, Z. and Avcı Öztürk, B. (2011), "Evaluation of salesperson candidates with fuzzy TOPSIS". Business and Economics Research Journal, 2(2), pp.77–100.

Büyüközkan, G. and Öztürkcan, D. (2010), "An integrated analytic approach for Six Sigma project selection". Expert Systems with Applications, 37(8), pp.5835–5847.

De Burgos Jiménez, J. and Cespedes Lorente, J. J. (2001), "Environmental performance as an operations objective". International Journal of Operations and Production Management, 21(12), pp.1553–1572.

Deif, A.M. (2011), "A system model for green manufacturing". Journal of Cleaner Production, 19(14), pp.1553–1559.

Del Brío, J.Á., and Junquera, B. (2003), "A review of the literature on environmental innovation management in SMEs: Implications for public policies". Technovation, 23(12), pp.939–948.

Dem, H., and Singh, S. R. (2015), "Joint replenishment modeling of a multi-item system with greening policy and volume flexibility". International Journal of Operational Research, 22(2), pp.148–166.

Fiksel, J. (1996), "Design for environment: Creating eco-efficient products and processes". McGraw-Hill.

Chapter 11

Green Manufacturing: A Comprehensive Exploration of Sustainable Practices and Industry 4.0 Integration

Hafiz Wasim Akram, Haidar Abbas, and Md. Daoud Ciddikie

11.1 Introduction

Manufacturing is essential to modern society because it creates jobs, stimulates the economy, and supplies essential goods and services (Rissman et al., 2020). However, conventional production methods often have negative effects on the environment, such as producing pollution, waste, and using up scarce resources. Green manufacturing has so arisen with the intention of lessening the negative effects of production on the natural world without sacrificing competitiveness. The phrase "green manufacturing" refers to the implementation of strategies that lessen the negative effects of production on the environment through time (Olah et al., 2020). Examples of such actions include reducing waste and pollution, increasing energy and resource efficiency, and favouring environmentally friendly products. The goal of "green manufacturing" is to create a production system that is both environmentally friendly and financially lucrative.

When it comes to solving the world's most pressing environmental problems, green manufacturing is crucial (Ahmadi et al., 2023). If we want

DOI: 10.4324/9781003439684-11

future generations to inherit a habitable planet, we must find solutions to pressing problems like climate change, pollution, and resource depletion. To address these challenges and keep up with societal demands for manufactured goods and services, green manufacturing is becoming increasingly vital (Ciliberto et al., 2021). Many governments and groups now promote and financially reward environmentally responsible production methods. The United Nations Sustainable Development Goals (SDGs) highlight the importance of sustainable production and consumption. Many governments are encouraging green manufacturing by providing tax exemptions and subsidies to companies that use eco-friendly policies and procedures (Khattak et al., 2022).

The environmental and economic benefits of green manufacturing are clear. Cost savings through reduced energy and resource use, enhanced brand reputation, and increased consumer demand for eco-friendly products are just a few of the many rewards for businesses that adopt sustainable manufacturing practices (Hegab et al., 2023). Additionally, companies that put an emphasis on sustainability are better able to adapt to changing regulations and consumer needs, hence reducing the likelihood of noncompliance and revenue loss. Many companies have been using environmentally friendly practices for decades (Abualfaraa et al., 2020), so the idea of "green manufacturing" is not novel. The Internet of Things (IoT) and artificial intelligence (AI) are only two examples of the recent technical developments that have opened up new opportunities for eco-friendly production. These innovations improve the efficacy of sustainable manufacturing by allowing for real-time monitoring, predictive maintenance, and optimization of resource and energy consumption.

11.2 Goal of Green Manufacturing

Green production, as everyone knows, is an approach to making goods with a focus on reducing the manufacturing sector's negative effects on the natural world. It is becoming increasingly important to include the principles of green manufacturing in industrial activities as the world faces the challenges of climate change and resource depletion (Bellezoni et al., 2022). The production process should aim to minimize its impact on the environment by cutting down on resource consumption, trash generation, and pollution emissions. Modifications to the design, production, and distribution phases are needed to reduce the environmental impact of manufacturing. Stakeholders in green manufacturing need to be convinced that it is essential for many reasons. For instance, it helps mitigate some of manufacturing's adverse effects on the natural world. By cutting down on waste and emissions, it can lessen the amount of pollution and damage to the environment from manufacturing. In addition to these benefits, green manufacturing can also boost the efficiency of the manufacturing process, saving money for businesses. Using less energy and raw materials can help manufacturers reduce manufacturing costs and increase competitiveness (Porter & Linde, 1995). In addition, consumers' increasing demand for eco-friendly products might be met with the aid of green manufacturing. More and more shoppers are looking for things that were made in a sustainable way as they become more aware of the negative effects their purchases have on the planet. Therefore, green manufacturing is essential to sustainable development because of the need to lessen the industry's negative influence on the environment, boost production efficiency, and keep up with rising consumer demand for eco-friendly goods. The goals of green manufacturing in broader terms can be categorized as shown in Figure 11.1.

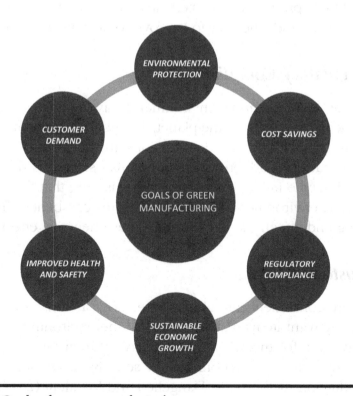

Figure 11.1   Goals of green manufacturing.

11.2.1 Environmental Protection

Conventional manufacturing techniques often have severe negative effects on the natural world. It requires substantial volumes of energy, water, and other natural resources (Aprianti, 2017). Greenhouse gases, poisonous chemicals, and hazardous waste are just some of the trash and pollution it generates. The effects of these toxins on ecosystems and human health are potentially catastrophic. They can impair soil quality, increase erosion, and decrease biodiversity. The goal of "green manufacturing" is to minimize waste, pollution, and the consumption of natural resources. This helps keep our planet safe and our natural resources intact for future generations.

11.2.2 Cost Savings

The goal of "green manufacturing" is to help businesses save a lot of money. Businesses may help the environment by reducing their consumption of energy and raw materials. This can help reduce overhead costs and boost profits (Maksimovic, 2018). Garbage disposal expenses can be extremely costly, but can be mitigated if firms produce less waste. The end goal of green manufacturing is to boost productivity and efficiency to improve competitiveness and profitability.

11.2.3 Regulatory Compliance

A growing body of international environmental law mandates that businesses reduce their negative effects on the planet. The goal of "green manufacturing" is to help companies follow these regulations and stay out of legal trouble. Organizations that don't adhere to environmental standards risk losing credibility and maybe facing legal action. By ensuring that their manufacturing process is environmentally compliant, firms can benefit from green manufacturing and lessen the likelihood of these negative effects.

11.2.4 Customer Demand

More and more consumers care about the ecological consequences of their purchases. They want items that are good for the environment, and they're willing to pay extra for them. Companies may set themselves apart from the competition and win over environmentally sensitive customers by switching to green production methods. As Dangelico and Vocalelli (2017) point out, this is a great way to boost brand loyalty and credibility with consumers.

11.2.5 Improved Health and Safety

Green manufacturing is an initiative that aims to boost the well-being of factory employees (Leso et al., 2018). Manufacturing processes that have been around for a while may expose workers to harmful chemicals and other pollutants. The goal of "green manufacturing" is to limit workers' exposure to potentially hazardous substances. The workplace may become safer and healthier as a result.

11.2.6 Sustainable Economic Growth

Sustainable economic growth depends on green manufacturing. A long-term objective, sustainable economic growth is to provide for the demands of the present without compromising the future prosperity of future generations. Green manufacturing practices aim to aid in this effort by decreasing the use of raw materials, cutting down on waste, and curbing the release of harmful by-products. Because of this, natural resources will be protected and the environment will be safe for future generations to enjoy.

11.3 Current Practices of Green Manufacturing

There are several reasons why green production is so important, and they are all readily apparent. It is essential for sustainability, financial savings, regulatory conformity, satisfying customers' needs, enhancing public health and safety, and boosting the economy in the long run. Businesses can improve their reputation with customers, increase productivity, and lessen their negative impact on the environment by adopting "green manufacturing" techniques. Conservation of natural resources and the availability of such resources for future generations are two additional benefits of green manufacturing. Current examples of environmentally friendly production methods include the following.

11.3.1 Using Renewable Energy Sources

Energy consumption and emissions of greenhouse gases (GHG) are both high in the manufacturing sector. In the last 20 years, businesses have realized they need to reduce their negative effects on the environment; thus, they have switched to renewable energy sources like solar, wind, and hydropower to run their operations (Rahman et al., 2022). Reduced greenhouse gas emissions and reliance on finite fossil fuels are only two of the many benefits of transitioning to renewable energy. One of the key reasons why manufacturers are switching to renewable energy sources is to reduce their carbon impact. Fossil fuels like coal, oil, and natural gas are the industry's primary energy sources. However, they contribute significantly to the release of greenhouse gases, a major driver of global warming. In order to reduce their impact on the environment and help mitigate the consequences of climate change, manufacturers can benefit from switching to renewable energy sources (Khan et al., 2020).

Hydropower, solar power, and other forms of renewable energy are decreasing in price as well. Inexpensive renewable energy sources like solar, wind, and hydro are becoming increasingly competitive. The cost of renewable energy sources has dropped below that of fossil fuels in many cases. Therefore, they are a good option for factories seeking to reduce their energy costs. Renewable energy sources have the added bonus of being easily deployable in close proximity to industrial facilities (Kabir et al., 2018). Wind turbines can be constructed on nearby property, and solar panels can be installed on the roofs of nearby factories. This reduces the potential for wasteful and expensive long-distance energy transmission across great distances. Energy independence and energy security are both improved when factories generate their own power rather than buying it from the utility company. Renewable power sources are more reliable than their fossil fuel counterparts. Energy availability and costs are vulnerable to market fluctuations and disruptions in the supply of fossil fuels. However, businesses may rely on a steady and reliable supply of energy from renewable sources because they are not affected by the same market dynamics. Renewable energy is becoming increasingly popular among manufacturers as a means of both reducing their environmental impact and conforming to new regulations (Liu, 2019). Greenhouse gas emission reduction targets have been set by several governments throughout the world, and manufacturers are feeling the pressure to comply. Using renewable energy sources allows manufacturers to reduce greenhouse gas emissions and maintain compliance with regulatory criteria as shown in Table 11.1.

There are promotional benefits to using renewable energy sources. Companies that can show they are committed to sustainability may gain an edge in a market where consumers are more worried about the impact of their purchases on the environment. Using renewable energy sources is one way for manufacturers to show they care about the environment and win over

Table 11.1   Current Practices of Green Manufacturing

S. No	Avenues	Usage Focus
1	Using renewable energy sources	Solar Power
		Wind Energy
		Hydropower
		Biomass Energy
2	Recycling and waste reduction	Waste Minimization
		Recycling Initiatives
		Resource Recovery
		Sustainable Material Management
3	Design for sustainability	Eco-design
		Sustainable Materials Selection
		Energy-Efficient Design
		Waste Reduction and Recycling
4	Energy-efficient production	Process Optimization
		Energy Monitoring and Control
		Renewable Energy Integration
5	Supply chain sustainability	Sustainable Sourcing
		Green Logistics
		Circular Supply Chain

Source: Based on literature review.

eco-conscious consumers. While there are many benefits to using renewable energy in manufacturing, there are also many downsides (Kabir et al., 2018). One of the main issues is that renewable energy sources tend to be intermittent. Renewable sources of power, such as solar and wind, are not always reliable because they rely on favorable weather conditions. This could create issues for businesses that rely on a steady supply of energy to function. Energy storage devices like batteries can help with this. Energy storage allows for the accumulation of renewable energy for later usage during times of low or no output. For manufacturing facilities, this means less reliance on costly and unreliable fossil fuels (Shahsavari & Akbari, 2018). The initial investment needed to develop the appropriate infrastructure is another problem with renewable energy. The initial investment in solar panels, wind turbines, and hydropower facilities can be challenging for some factories to bear. In the long run, however, this investment may prove worthwhile if it helps reduce energy prices and improve energy security.

11.3.2 Recycling and Waste Reduction

As the globe struggles to deal with the growing worry of climate change, manufacturing companies are expanding their efforts to reduce waste and recycle materials. This is a good commercial practise as well as a responsible one for the environment. By reducing waste and finding new uses for old products, businesses can save money, conserve resources, and reduce their environmental impact. Packaging waste reduction strategies are one method manufacturers are using to cut down on waste (Rubio et al., 2019). Lighter, more eco-friendly materials, innovative packaging designs, and recycling initiatives are all part of this strategy. For instance, Procter & Gamble, a global leader in consumer goods, has committed to eliminating all landfill disposal of manufacturing waste by the year 2030. In order to accomplish this, the organization is creating initiatives to lessen packaging waste and increase recycling rates. One way that P&G is reducing its plastic footprint is by switching to a new packaging design for its Tide brand (Agarwal & Thiel, 2013).

To further reduce waste, manufacturers are increasingly turning to resource recycling. Products made with recycled materials, goods designed for reuse, and closed-loop technologies in which resources are reused throughout the production process all fall under this category (Jawahir & Bradley, 2016). IKEA, a Swedish furniture manufacturer, has made a number of products out of recycled materials, such as a range of kitchen cabinets made out of plastic bottles (Lacy et al., 2020). The company is also reusing waste materials as raw materials by utilizing closed-loop technologies in its production processes. Companies are beginning to implement recycling programs for common materials including metals, plastics, and paper. Materials from their own operations are collected and recycled, and closed-loop supply chains are developed in collaboration with customers and vendors (Schenkel et al., 2015). For instance, Alcoa has developed a closed-loop method for aluminum can production in which recycled cans are fed back into the same assembly process. This method reduces the business's ecological footprint by preventing unnecessary waste and conserving useful resources.

11.3.3 Design for Sustainability

Incorporating sustainability ideas into product design is becoming increasingly important to manufacturers. Products should be made to endure as long as possible, be easily repaired and recycled, and use as little materials as possible. Businesses may decrease their negative effects on the environment by cutting down on waste and conserving resources. Use of high-quality materials and an emphasis on repairability and maintenance ease are key. For instance, outdoor clothing producer Patagonia has developed a range of wear-resistant, mendable garments (Lee et al., 2017). Customers who would otherwise throw away worn or torn garments can instead send them to the company for repair. Patagonia encourages a culture of sustainability among its patrons by creating products that may be repaired rather than thrown away. Manufacturers are incorporating sustainability ideas into product development by producing recyclable products. Aluminum, glass, and some types of plastics are all examples of recyclable materials that can be used for this purpose. Apple, a tech company, has promised to make all of its products entirely out of recycled materials (Dauvergne & Lister, 2013). Apple has already made substantial headway toward this goal by using recycled aluminum in several of its products and inventing a robot called Daisy that can disassemble and recover elements from outdated iPhones. Apple's efforts to decrease waste and preserve natural resources begin with the company's product designs.

The amount of raw resources used in manufactured goods is decreasing. This includes the use of more resource-efficient materials and the development of products that use less resources overall. According to a 2017 study by Moorhouse and Moorhouse, Adidas has developed a range of footwear out of marine debris. In addition, the "Better Cotton" initiative has been implemented to encourage environmentally friendly methods of cotton production and to lessen the company's dependence on external water sources (Vadicherla & Saravanan, 2015). Adidas is preserving resources and minimizing waste by cutting back on the amount of materials used in production.

11.3.4 Energy-Efficient Production

Because of growing awareness of the negative environmental effects of their operations, manufacturers are taking a variety of steps to cut down on energy use and greenhouse gas emissions. This includes the implementation of water-saving practices and the implementation of energy-saving technology and procedures. Manufacturers are integrating energy-efficient technology by modernizing their equipment. GM has introduced energy management systems to monitor and optimize energy usage in its facilities, reducing energy consumption and greenhouse gas emissions (Eckert et al., 2021). This involves replacing old and inefficient equipment with newer, more efficient models. These measures have helped General Motors get closer to its goal of decreasing its energy intensity. Another way factories cut back on energy use is by switching to sustainable energy sources like solar and wind power. The Swedish furniture giant IKEA has been using renewable energy to power its business since it began installing solar panels on the tops of its stores and distribution hubs (Alrubah et al., 2020). Using renewable energy sources, IKEA lowers its reliance on fossil fuels and its emissions of greenhouse gases.

Water conservation practices are being adopted by factories alongside energy efficiency initiatives. Precipitation harvesting, water recycling infrastructure construction, and manufacturing techniques that use less water all fall under this category. Levi Strauss & Co., a clothing manufacturer, has, for instance, installed a water recycling system at its factory in Mexico (Amutha, 2017). Because the system cleans and reuses wastewater, less fresh water is used in the manufacturing process. Levi's has installed low-flow faucets and lavatories at their worldwide sites as part of an effort to reduce water usage. Because of these efforts, Levi's factories have cut their water use by 96%. Coca-Cola is another industry pioneer when it comes to saving water. The beverage manufacturer has started a campaign to recycle the water they use in manufacturing back into the ecosystem. Coca-Cola's bottling plants have been using less water due to the installation of water-saving technology since 2004. Coca-Cola was able to accomplish their goal thanks to these efforts.

11.3.5 Supply Chain Sustainability

Suppliers' adoption of environmentally responsible methods is becoming increasingly important to manufacturers who are increasingly aware of the need to minimize their own environmental effect. This includes things like picking vendors based on how well they do in terms of sustainability and working with them to improve their operations. In order to assess and rank their suppliers' sustainability performance, major athletic footwear and clothing maker Nike has created a plan (Porteous & Rammohan, 2013). Suppliers are ranked on their commitment to social and environmental responsibility in Nike's Sustainable Manufacturing and Sourcing Index. Nike also aims to improve its suppliers' sustainability practices by offering training and tools to bring them up to par with Nike's own high sustainability standards. Manufacturers are working with their suppliers to improve their sustainable practices by implementing sustainability initiatives in their supply chains. To measure the sustainability performance of their vendors, major retailer Walmart created a program called the Sustainability Index (Cowan et al., 2010). Suppliers' environmental and social sustainability practices are assessed, and recommendations and tools are offered to help them improve. Walmart also provides its suppliers with support as they adopt sustainable practices like recycling and lowering their carbon footprint.

In addition to carefully selecting and working with suppliers, manufacturers are implementing programs to improve the sustainability of their supply chains. For instance, Unilever, a multinational manufacturer and marketer of consumer goods, has launched a project called the Sustainable Living Plan (Murphy & Murphy, 2018). The strategy sets lofty targets for Unilever's sustainability performance, such as cutting their environmental impact and helping workers in its supply chain live better lives. Together with its suppliers, Unilever works to implement sustainable practices like cutting down on water use and carbon emissions. Patagonia, a maker of outdoor gear, is also working to green their supply chain. Patagonia's Footprint Chronicles initiative details the materials used and the facilities that produce their items to reduce their negative impact on the environment (Rattalino, 2018). When it comes to environmental responsibility, Patagonia works with its vendors to improve their procedures.

11.4 Future of Green Manufacturing in Correlation With Industry 4.0

To reduce the negative effects on the environment caused by production, "green manufacturing" uses eco-friendly techniques and materials. Artificial intelligence, the Internet of Things, and automation are hallmarks of Industry 4.0, and they have important repercussions for the future of environmentally friendly production. Industry 4.0, the adoption of cutting-edge technology like AI and the IoT in production, has significant positive benefits on environmentally friendly production (Ashima et al., 2021). One of the most notable benefits is the increased opportunity for data collection and analysis throughout the manufacturing process. Manufacturing processes may be optimized to reduce waste and boost efficiency, and energy and resource consumption can be lowered by using this data to pinpoint problem areas. Real-time information on energy and water use can be gathered with the help of sensors and other monitoring devices (Koo et al., 2015). By analyzing this data, it will be possible to spot problem areas and implement solutions, such as cutting down on energy use and garbage. Manufacturers may enhance both their bottom line and their influence on the environment by making use of data-driven insights to optimize production processes. For instance, manufacturing companies can cut their energy use and associated expenses by pinpointing locations where improvements might be made. Manufacturers may lessen their negative effects on the environment and their bottom lines by cutting back on trash production and disposal costs. Data analysis can guide the development of both new products and production techniques and the improvement of existing ones. By examining data on product perform-ance and customer input, manufacturers can find ways to increase product sustainability, such as by utilizing more environmentally friendly materials or designing items for easier disassembly and recycling.

The ability to gather and examine massive amounts of data is a powerful tool for environmentally responsible production. Manufacturers may lessen their negative effect on the environment and boost their bottom line and competitiveness by using data to optimize processes and produce more sustainable goods (Rosen & Kishawy, 2012). Industry 4.0 can help green production in many ways, including the use of automation and robotics. Using automation and robotics, Industry 4.0 can also help green manufac-turing. Automated procedures have the potential to be more precise and efficient than their manual counterparts, cutting down on both waste and energy use. The use of 3D printing to create parts with little waste and the employment of robots to enhance assembly operations can both help cut down on energy use. Automation and robots are used in green manufacturing in the production of electric vehicles. Electric car manufacture requires precise manufacturing procedures and lightweight materials to maximize energy efficiency. The production of electric automobiles can have a smaller carbon footprint if automated manufacturing procedures are used (Nascimento et al., 2019). Automation and robotics are also used in the production of solar panels, another form of green manufacturing. Manufacturing solar panels requires strong but lightweight materials and careful attention to detail. Using automated manufacturing methods can improve the efficiency and reduce the waste in the manufacture of solar panels, which in turn will have a positive effect on the environment.

The use of automation and robotics in factories has the potential to improve working conditions, as well as decrease waste and boost productivity. For instance, robots can be utilized to undertake dangerous or repetitive tasks, lowering the risk of harm to human workers. As a result, this can boost morale and safety in factories, leading to a more environmentally and socially responsible production process (Ben-Ari et al., 2018). The use of automation and robotics is crucial to sustainable production in the age of Industry 4.0. Through decreased waste, increased productivity, and better working conditions, automation and robotics can help make production more environmentally and socially responsible.

By equipping manufacturers with cutting-edge resources that enhance both the design and manufacturing phases, Industry 4.0 can speed up the creation of new eco-friendly materials and goods (Javaid et al., 2022). Manufacturers can reduce their environmental effect by making use of biodegradable or recycled materials with the help of 3D printing technology. Manufacturers may reduce stock and waste by producing items as needed using 3D printing technology. Another way in which Industry 4.0 contributes to environmentally friendly product creation is through the development of smart devices. Sensors and an internet connection provide smart items the ability to monitor and report on their own performance and usage. This data can improve the product's energy efficiency and overall performance by informing future design and manufacturing decisions.

Furthermore, Industry 4.0 can pave the way for the development of new sustainable business models (Onu & Mbohwa, 2021). For instance, product-as-a-service models encourage producers to make items that last a long time and are simple to fix, lowering their overall environmental footprint. In this model, the original equipment manufacturer (OEM) is responsible for a product's upkeep and replacement parts throughout its useful life. In this way, the manufacturer is incentivized to make products that last and require minimal upkeep, cutting down on waste. Industry 4.0 has made possible several sustainable business models, such as the circular economy concept. The circular economic model is a self-sustaining system in which materials are reused for as long as possible, hence preserving their value and reducing waste. Industry 4.0 has the potential to pave the way for a circular economy by equipping factories with the means to maximize resource utilization, enhance product durability and recycling, and set up self-sustaining, closed-loop supply chains. Since this is the case, Industry 4.0 may help pave the way for more eco-friendly materials, goods, and even businesses (de Man & Strandhagen, 2017). Using cutting-edge equipment and technologies, producers may make goods that are better for the planet, society, and the bottom line.

But there are also difficulties for green production in the age of Industry 4.0. One of the biggest problems could be an increase in energy use from implementing new technologies. For example, running AI and machine learning algorithms requires a lot of processing power, which might increase energy usage. Companies like Google are facing this problem head-on. The corporation has made significant investments in AI and machine learning, which necessitate a large amount of computational power. In response, Google has implemented a number of measures to cut down on its energy usage and carbon output. For instance, Google has invested heavily in renewable energy projects with the aim of deriving all of its energy needs (Urs Hölzle, 2016). The business has decreased its energy use through measures such as the installation of data centers and refrigeration systems that use less power. Amazon, like many other IT giants, has taken heat for the amount of power its cloud services use. In response, the firm has committed significant resources to renewable energy projects with the goal of reaching net-zero carbon emissions by 2040 (Li et al., 2022). To further lower its carbon footprint, Amazon has used serverless computing in addition to other energy-saving technologies (Ko et al., 2021). While it's true that cutting-edge electronics could increase energy usage, many companies are instead making investments in green power and energy-saving innovations.

Another challenge is that the employment of cutting-edge technology may lead to more electronic waste (Gangisetti et al., 2023) than is currently the case. There may be an increase in e-waste when firms adopt new technology and render existing ones obsolete. Sustainable e-waste management practices should be used by manufacturers to reduce the negative effects of modern technologies on the environment. Apple is one corporation that has taken steps to reduce its e-waste production (Marke et al., 2020). The Apple Trade In plan is a thorough effort on the part of the corporation to recycle old Apple hardware. Customers can get store credit toward the purchase of new Apple devices by trading in their dated products through this promotion. Apple uses aluminum from recycled cans in its MacBook Air and Mac mini, among other items. Also, Dell has created a closed-loop recycling strategy for its products. Dell's plan collects and recycles old items and components in order to make room for brand-new ones in the manufacturing process (Gong et al., 2022). In addition, Dell has aimed to use 100 million pounds of recycled material by 2030 (Vadakkepatt et al., 2021). Manufacturers will need to employ sustainable e-waste management practices to decrease the environmental impact of modern technology as their use continues to expand. Companies like Apple and Dell are the vanguard of implementing these practices, but for them to have any lasting impact, others will need to follow suit.

As a result, green manufacturing faces both opportunities and challenges as a result of the incorporation of Industry 4.0 technology. While increasing efficiency, decreasing waste, and facilitating the creation of new, sustainable materials and products, advanced technologies nevertheless have the potential to increase energy consumption and e-waste. Manufacturers will need to implement sustainable practices to reduce the negative effects of these technologies on the environment while still reaping the benefits of Industry 4.0.

11.5 Conclusion

The importance of eco-friendly industrial practices in today's factories is growing daily. The goal of sustainability is driven not only by environmental concerns, but also by economic considerations, as manufacturers see the potential cost reductions associated with lowering waste and energy use. Without adopting environmentally responsible production methods, SDGs 9 (industry, innovation, and infrastructure), 12 (responsible consumption and production), and 13 (climate action) would never be realized. Current green manufacturing practices place an emphasis on minimizing waste and energy use, designing with sustainability in mind, employing energy-efficient technologies, conserving water resources, and working with vendors to promote similar initiatives. Many companies throughout the world have already benefited from the decreased costs, increased productivity, and improved sustainability performance that resulted from adopting these practices.

Industry 4.0 technologies are widely expected to lead to ever more environmentally friendly production processes. The Internet of Things (IoT), artificial intelligence (AI), machine learning (ML), and robotics are all examples of Industry 4.0 technologies with the potential to collect and analyze large amounts of data from manufacturing processes, optimize those processes to reduce waste and increase efficiency, and pave the way for the creation of new, more eco-friendly materials and products. Problems, such as higher energy usage and more e-waste production, are posed by the widespread use of these technologies, however. It will be vital for manufacturers to overcome these challenges and employ ecologically acceptable practices to ensure the long-term success of these technologies.

11.6 Summary and Future Directions

The future of environmentally responsible production is likely to be shaped by a number of current tendencies. Some examples are using renewable energy, creating new sustainable materials and goods, incorporating sustainability into corporate models, and adopting circular economy ideas. The circular economy is a policy that promotes resource reuse and deters waste. Closed-loop systems for resource utilization and waste management are put into place, and long-lasting, repairable, and recyclable product designs are developed. It is predicted that the widespread implementation of circular economy concepts will increase investment in green manufacturing and lead to the development of more environmentally friendly production processes. Renewable energy is expected to play a pivotal role in the development of eco-friendly production in the years to come. Manufacturers may cut their consumption of fossil fuels and their contribution to global warming by utilizing renewable energy sources like solar, wind, and others. It is anticipated that the development of new sustainable materials and products would quicken as manufacturers work to lessen their environmental effect and satisfy consumer demand for sustainable goods. Companies are increasingly recognizing the environmental and financial benefits of adopting sustainable business models like product-as-a-service models.

Eco-friendly production techniques are crucial for a sustainable future. Reducing waste and energy consumption, incorporating sustainability principles into product design, implementing energy-efficient technologies, conserving water, and working with suppliers to ensure they are also implementing sustainable practices are currently regarded as the most important aspects of green manufacturing. Although widespread implementation of Industry 4.0 technologies is expected to enhance these procedures, there are still obstacles to be overcome to ensure their long-term survival. It is expected that the incorporation of circular economy ideas, the utilization of renewable energy sources, the creation of new sustainable materials and products, and the adoption of sustainability in business models will all define the future of green manufacturing. The SDGs and a sustainable future for all depend on the continued implementation of green industrial practices.

References

Abualfaraa, W., Salonitis, K., Al-Ashaab, A., & Ala'raj, M. (2020). Lean-green manufacturing practices and their link with sustainability: A critical review. *Sustainability*, *12*(3), 981.

Ahmadi, M., Rahmatabadi, D., Karimi, A., Koohpayeh, M. H. A., & Hashemi, R. (2023). The role of additive manufacturing in the age of sustainable manufacturing 4.0. In *Sustainable manufacturing in industry 4.0: Pathways and practices* (pp. 57–78). Singapore: Springer Nature Singapore.

Agarwal, R., & Thiel, M. (2013). P&G: Providing sustainable innovative products through LCA worldwide. *South Asian Journal of Business and Management Cases, 2*(1), 85–96.

Alrubah, S. A., Alsubaie, L. K., Quttainah, M. A., Pal, M., Pandey, R., Kee, D. M. H., … & Aishan, N. (2020). Factors affecting environmental performance: A study of IKEA. *International Journal of Tourism and Hospitality in Asia Pacific (IJTHAP), 3*(3), 79–89.

Amutha, K. (2017). Environmental impacts of denim. In *Sustainability in denim* (pp. 27–48). Woodhead Publishing.

Aprianti, E. (2017). A huge number of artificial waste material can be supplementary cementitious material (SCM) for concrete production–a review part II. *Journal of Cleaner Production, 142*, 4178–4194.

Ashima, R., Haleem, A., Bahl, S., Javaid, M., Mahla, S. K., & Singh, S. (2021). Automation and manufacturing of smart materials in additive manufacturing technologies using Internet of Things toward the adoption of Industry 4.0. *Materials Today: Proceedings, 45*, 5081–5088.

Bellezoni, R. A., Seto, K. C., & Puppim de Oliveira, J. A. (2022). What can cities do to enhance water-energy-food nexus as a sustainable development strategy?. In *Water-energy-food nexus and climate change in cities* (pp. 39–57). Cham: Springer International Publishing.

Ben-Ari, M., Mondada, F., Ben-Ari, M., & Mondada, F. (2018). Robots and their applications. *Elements of Robotics*, 1–20.

Ciliberto, C., Szopik-Depczyńska, K., Tarczyńska-Łuniewska, M., Ruggieri, A., & Ioppolo, G. (2021). Enabling the Circular Economy transition: A sustainable lean manufacturing recipe for Industry 4.0. *Business Strategy and the Environment, 30*(7), 3255–3272.

Cowan, D. M., Dopart, P., Ferracini, T., Sahmel, J., Merryman, K., Gaffney, S., & Paustenbach, D. J. (2010). A cross-sectional analysis of reported corporate environmental sustainability practices. *Regulatory Toxicology and Pharmacology, 58*(3), 524–538.

Dangelico, R. M., & Vocalelli, D. (2017). "Green Marketing": An analysis of definitions, strategy steps, and tools through a systematic review of the literature. *Journal of Cleaner Production, 165*, 1263–1279.

Dauvergne, P., & Lister, J. (2013). *Eco-business: A big-brand takeover of sustainability*. MIT Press.

de Man, J. C., & Strandhagen, J. O. (2017). An Industry 4.0 research agenda for sustainable business models. *Procedia Cirp, 63*, 721–726.

Eckert, J. J., da Silva, S. F., de Menezes Lourenço, M. A., Correa, F. C., Silva, L. C., & Dedini, F. G. (2021). Energy management and gear shifting control for a hybridized vehicle to minimize gas emissions, energy consumption and battery aging. *Energy Conversion and Management, 240*, 114222.

Gangisetti, S., Sahu, R. K., & Parihar, R. S. (2023). Challenges in green waste-reinforced aluminum composites. *Waste Residue Composites, 16*, 163.

Gong, Y., Wang, Y., Frei, R., Wang, B., & Zhao, C. (2022). Blockchain application in circular marine plastic debris management. *Industrial Marketing Management, 102*, 164–176.

Hegab, H., Shaban, I., Jamil, M., & Khanna, N. (2023). Toward sustainable future: Strategies, indicators, and challenges for implementing sustainable production systems. *Sustainable Materials and Technologies, 36*, e00617.

Javaid, M., Haleem, A., Singh, R. P., Suman, R., & Gonzalez, E. S. (2022). Understanding the adoption of Industry 4.0 technologies in improving environmental sustainability. *Sustainable Operations and Computers*.

Jawahir, I. S., & Bradley, R. (2016). Technological elements of circular economy and the principles of 6R-based closed-loop material flow in sustainable manufacturing. *Procedia Cirp, 40*, 103–108.

Kabir, E., Kumar, P., Kumar, S., Adelodun, A. A., & Kim, K. H. (2018). Solar energy: Potential and future prospects. *Renewable and Sustainable Energy Reviews, 82*, 894–900.

Khan, H., Khan, I., & Binh, T. T. (2020). The heterogeneity of renewable energy consumption, carbon emission and financial development in the globe: A panel quantile regression approach. *Energy Reports, 6*, 859–867.

Khattak, S. I., Ahmad, M., ul Haq, Z., Shaofu, G., & Hang, J. (2022). On the goals of sustainable production and the conditions of environmental sustainability: Does cyclical innovation in green and sustainable technologies determine carbon dioxide emissions in G-7 economies. *Sustainable Production and Consumption, 29*, 406–420.

Ko, H., Pack, S., & Leung, V. C. (2021). Performance optimization of serverless computing for latency-guaranteed and energy-efficient task offloading in energy harvesting industrial IoT. *IEEE Internet of Things Journal*.

Koo, D., Piratla, K., & Matthews, C. J. (2015). Toward sustainable water supply: Schematic development of big data collection using internet of things (IoT). *Procedia Engineering, 118*, 489–497.

Lacy, P., Long, J., & Spindler, W. (2020). *The circular economy handbook* (Vol. 259). London: Palgrave Macmillan UK.

Lee, M. S., Seifert, M., & Cherrier, H. (2017). Anti-consumption and governance in the global fashion industry: Transparency is key. *Governing Corporate Social Responsibility in the Apparel Industry after Rana Plaza*, 147–174.

Leso, V., Fontana, L., & Iavicoli, I. (2018). The occupational health and safety dimension of Industry 4.0. *La Medicina del lavoro, 109*(5), 327.

Li, K., Acha, S., Sunny, N., & Shah, N. (2022). Strategic transport fleet analysis of heavy goods vehicle technology for net-zero targets. *Energy Policy, 168*, 112988.

Liu, J. (2019). China's renewable energy law and policy: A critical review. *Renewable and Sustainable Energy Reviews, 99*, 212–219.

Maksimovic, M. (2018). Greening the future: Green Internet of Things (G-IoT) as a key technological enabler of sustainable development. *Internet of things and big data analytics toward next-generation intelligence*, 283–313.

Marke, A., Chan, C., Taskin, G., & Hacking, T. (2020). Reducing e-waste in China's mobile electronics industry: the application of the innovative circular business models. *Asian Education and Development Studies*, *9*(4), 591–610.

Moorhouse, D., & Moorhouse, D. (2017). Sustainable Design: Circular economy in fashion and textiles. *The Design Journal*, *20*(sup1), S1948–S1959.

Murphy, P. E., & Murphy, C. E. (2018). Sustainable living: Unilever. *Progressive Business Models: Creating Sustainable and Pro-social Enterprise*, 263–286.

Nascimento, D. L. M., Alencastro, V., Quelhas, O. L. G., Caiado, R. G. G., Garza-Reyes, J. A., Rocha-Lona, L., & Tortorella, G. (2019). Exploring Industry 4.0 technologies to enable circular economy practices in a manufacturing context: A business model proposal. *Journal of Manufacturing Technology Management*, *30*(3), 607–627.

Oláh, J., Aburumman, N., Popp, J., Khan, M. A., Haddad, H., & Kitukutha, N. (2020). Impact of Industry 4.0 on environmental sustainability. *Sustainability*, *12*(11), 4674.

Onu, P., & Mbohwa, C. (2021). Industry 4.0 opportunities in manufacturing SMEs: Sustainability outlook. *Materials Today: Proceedings*, *44*, 1925–1930.

Porteous, A., & Rammohan, S. (2013). Integration, incentives and innovation Nike's strategy to improve social and environmental conditions in its global supply chain. *Stanford Institute for the Study of Supply Chain Responsibility, Stanford, CA*.

Porter, M., & Van der Linde, C. (1995). Green and competitive: Ending the stalemate. *The Dynamics of the Eco-efficient Economy: Environmental Regulation and Competitive Advantage*, *33*, 120–134.

Rahman, A., Farrok, O., & Haque, M. M. (2022). Environmental impact of renewable energy source based electrical power plants: Solar, wind, hydroelectric, biomass, geothermal, tidal, ocean, and osmotic. *Renewable and Sustainable Energy Reviews*, *161*, 112279.

Rattalino, F. (2018). Circular advantage anyone? Sustainability-driven innovation and circularity at Patagonia, Inc. *Thunderbird International Business Review*, *60*(5), 747–755.

Rissman, J., Bataille, C., Masanet, E., Aden, N., Morrow III, W. R., Zhou, N., ... & Helseth, J. (2020). Technologies and policies to decarbonize global industry: Review and assessment of mitigation drivers through 2070. *Applied Energy*, *266*, 114848.

Rosen, M. A., & Kishawy, H. A. (2012). Sustainable manufacturing and design: Concepts, practices and needs. *Sustainability*, *4*(2), 154–174.

Rubio, S., Ramos, T. R. P., Leitão, M. M. R., & Barbosa-Povoa, A. P. (2019). Effectiveness of extended producer responsibility policies implementation: The case of Portuguese and Spanish packaging waste systems. *Journal of Cleaner Production*, *210*, 217–230.

Schenkel, M., Krikke, H., Caniëls, M. C., & van der Laan, E. (2015). Creating integral value for stakeholders in closed loop supply chains. *Journal of Purchasing and Supply Management*, *21*(3), 155–166.

Shahsavari, A., & Akbari, M. (2018). Potential of solar energy in developing countries for reducing energy-related emissions. *Renewable and Sustainable Energy Reviews*, *90*, 275–291.

Urs Hölzle (2016). 00% renewable is just the beginning. https://sustainability.google/progress/projects/announcement-100/

Vadakkepatt, G. G., Winterich, K. P., Mittal, V., Zinn, W., Beitelspacher, L., Aloysius, J., ... & Reilman, J. (2021). Sustainable retailing. *Journal of Retailing*, *97*(1), 62–80.

Vadicherla, T., & Saravanan, D. (2015). Sustainable measures taken by brands, retailers, and manufacturers. *Roadmap to Sustainable Textiles and Clothing: Regulatory Aspects and Sustainability Standards of Textiles and the Clothing Supply Chain*, 109–135.

Index

Note: page numbers in **bold** refer to tables and *italics* refer to figures

Printed in the United States
by Baker & Taylor Publisher Services